JACK WELCH
AND LEADERSHIP

JACK WELCH AND LEADERSHIP

Executive Lessons
of the Master CEO

J A M E S   W .   R O B I N S O N

FORUM
An Imprint of Prima Publishing

Published by Prima Publishing, Roseville, California. Member of the
Crown Publishing Group, a division of Random House, Inc.

Random House, Inc. New York, Toronto, London, Sydney, Auckland

PRIMA PUBLISHING, FORUM, and colophons are trademarks of Random
House, Inc., registered with the United States Patent and Trademark Office.

Library of Congress Cataloging-in-Publication Data on file.

ISBN 0-7615-3545-4

01 02 03 04 05 HH 10 9 8 7 6 5 4 3 2 1
Printed in the United States of America

First Edition

Visit us online at www.primaforum.com

CONTENTS

ACKNOWLEDGMENTS

Books are never really written by just one person. I had a great deal of help and support. Thanks especially to Tom Donohue, Rita Bond, Duc Nguyen—and the friendly hotel staffs in Honolulu, Tokyo, and Bangkok, where much of the manuscript was drafted.

I am also indebted to the great team at Prima Publishing, including David Richardson and Andrew Vallas.

JACK WELCH
AND LEADERSHIP

CHAPTER 1

JACK WELCH AND THE MAKING OF THE BUSINESS LEADER

The task of a leader is to get his people from where
they are to where they have not been.
—HENRY KISSINGER

AMERICANS LOOK in many places for heroes, role models, and leaders. Sports, entertainment, politics, diplomacy, war, medicine, and the arts have all provided men and women we look up to and learn from. Largely neglected have been the leaders of American business—despite the fact that over the past century dozens of business leaders have, as Henry Kissinger prescribed, collectively taken the American people to places they have never been—to levels of prosperity, personal comfort, opportunity, and quality of life never before known in human history.

One of those leaders is Jack Welch, outgoing chairman and CEO of General Electric. He is a man who rose from a modest background to lead one of the world's greatest business institutions—an ordinary man who achieved extraordinary things. Powered by a few simple business principles, the courage to make big decisions, an inexhaustible supply of energy and self-confidence, and a 100 percent dedication to his company and the people in it, Welch transformed GE into the most valuable company in America and a global economic powerhouse.

In doing so, he did not personally invent new products like Thomas Alva Edison or Steve Jobs. He did not pioneer revolutionary technologies like William Shockley or Bill Gates. He did not create a business behemoth out of his garage like Henry Ford or William Hewlett and David Packard. Nor did he use his business success to build new platforms and movements in other arenas like Lee Iacocca or H. Ross Perot.

Jack Welch was and is the quintessential organization man, someone who climbed the corporate ladder rung by rung. But unlike other organization men or women, he saw each rung, including the one at the very top, as part of a journey, not a destination—and he pulled many others up with him each step of the way. His distinctive contribution has been to transform the role of manager into that of leader and to remind us all that if you're in the leadership business, first and foremost you're in the people business.

By leading GE instead of managing it, and by focusing most of his time and energy on people rather than appliances, jet engines, or the Thursday night lineup on NBC, Welch took a company that many believed had already reached the top rung on the ladder and made it build a whole new ladder to climb.

- In 1981 (the year Welch took over) sales per employee totaled $69,000. By the end of his tenure, they reached $382,000.

- In 1981 market capitalization was $13 billion. On the eve of his departure, it was $494 billion.

- In 1981 revenues were $28 billion. In 2000 revenues totaled $130 billion.

- GE stock traded at nine times earnings in 1981. In 2000, the company's price-earnings ratio was 40 to 1.

- Shareholders who bought stock in 1980 have seen a total compounded annual return of 23 percent under Welch. Since his April 1, 1981, start date as CEO, the stock has climbed 3,000 percent—compared with 896 percent for the S&P as a whole.

- In 1981 less than 20 percent of company revenues were derived from overseas operations. Under Welch international business grew to generate 41 percent of revenues. Revenues from service businesses such GE Capital moved from a minority share to a majority of the company's revenues.

- In 2000 *Fortune* named General Electric the most admired corporation in America for the fourth year running, while the *Financial Times* named it the most admired company in the world for the fourth time. *Fortune* named Welch "Manager of the Century" in 1999.

Welch did many things right in his almost unheard of 20-year run as chairman and CEO. He also made decisions that turned out to be questionable or wrong. Failures as well as successes offer lessons in leadership—lessons that can be applied not only to leadership in business but to aspiring leaders in all fields as well as in daily life.

Readers will find in these pages neither a puff piece nor an exposé, but an interpretative exploration that derives instruction and inspiration not only from what Jack Welch said but from who he is, what he represents, and the examples he has set. It is for this reason that I have not attempted to interview Welch for this book, nor have I relied only upon his own pronouncements on leadership. My goal has been to extrapolate from the life and career of the world's premier contemporary business leader, from his triumphs and disappointments, useful guidance and insights for others seeking professional success or charged with leading groups or organizations of all sizes.

FOOTSTEPS WORTH FOLLOWING?

THERE ARE THOSE who dicount the idea of a businessperson serving as a positive role model for the broader society. "GE is just a company, albeit a very successful one," wrote analyst Andy Serwer in the February 19, 2001, issue of *Fortune*. "And Welch is just a CEO, albeit a very good one. Let's just leave it at that."[1] An executive at a major transportation company seemed to share this blasé view when I asked him to assess Welch. "The culture of GE has produced thousands of very fine managers over the years, one of which was Jack Welch," he commented.

The notion that we should neither ask nor expect anything more of business leaders than that they "take care of business" has been a common one throughout much of our history. The idea of businesspeople fulfilling the role of legend or role model simply doesn't resonate with most citizens. On the contrary, as globalization of the economy proceeds apace, many choose instead to see our top executives as villains—amoral, exploitative forces who suck wealth and resources from workers and societies around the world for their own aggrandizement.

The most extreme of these views can be regarded as a by-product of their purveyors' intractable anticapitalist ideology. For those who are more typically nonideological, their reticence to embrace the business leader as one worth learning from and emulating is curious.

Why? It is easy to speculate. To all but the most obsessive business junkies, there seems to be a distinct lack of drama in what our captains of industry do. They are colorless and emotionless—mostly late-middle-aged, balding or graying white men in blue suits, busy laying people off and worrying about their golf game. Most are too tied up with the day-to-day dictates of management to communicate their achievements or their viewpoints in a compelling way. (As one who came up through the professional ranks writing speeches I can assure you that very accomplished corporate chiefs—people who actually have a rich fund of insights and ideas to share—are often among the worst speechmakers in any field.)

Or perhaps our love/hate relationship with capitalism, money, and the profit motive explains our off-putting attitude toward business leaders. There's nothing intrinsically heroic about the pursuit of wealth—even though most of us are endlessly dreaming of ways to acquire more of it. Except for family, money is the bottom line for most people—we just don't like to admit it and we're uncomfortable putting on a pedestal those who seem to epitomize the pursuit of the Almighty Dollar.

Most don't seem to care very much that top sports and television figures now earn hundreds of thousands of dollars for a single game or TV shoot—but they huff and puff in indignation upon hearing that the CEO of a big company may earn 30 times more than the guy on the shop floor. What we won't hear from the corporate community is that such a CEO probably has at least 30 times more responsibility, in terms of impact on society and the lives of the company's workers, investors, and customers, and therefore deserves every cent and probably more. They're afraid we'll shoot the messenger for telling us something we simply don't want to believe could possibly be true. It runs counter to the strong egalitarian impulse running through our culture and history.

Or perhaps the reluctance to embrace businesspeople as icons is because many believe they see big CEOs amassing enormous power and coldly making decisions that affect real people's lives with only the bottom line as their moral compass—and all with few checks and balances. As much as we celebrate, for example, heroes in sports, and see in their lives lessons to learn and values to follow, the fact is they have no real practical impact on our daily lives. They inspire and they excite and the world would be a dreary place without them— but whether they win or lose, triumph or choke, has no impact on the average person. Yet every day we see companies and their leaders making decisions that affect everyday people for better or for worse. So we're more critical, more probing, and less prone to fantasy in our assessments.

THE BUSINESS LEADER REAL AND IMAGINED

IN THE UNITED STATES, business leaders have occasionally captured the imagination and attention of the public. During the Gilded Age of the late 19th century, those who did were feared, scorned, and seen as epitomizing all that was wrong with society.

Writing in *Forbes' American Heritage* magazine in October 1998, John Steele Gordon explains, "That image of the businessman was formed at the turn of the century, when Americans were piling up fortunes of unprecedented scale in the Industrial Revolution and the left was a rising force in American politics, calling for increased government supervision of business. Such historians as Ida Tarbell, Gustavus Meyers, Upton Sinclair, and Mathew Josephson depicted all these men as ruthless, diabolical, power-mad automatons of greed."[2]

Yet in the early years of the 20th century several business pioneers did achieve more positive images, even folk hero status—giants such as Edison, Ford, and the Wright brothers stand out. But their reputations were built primarily on their participation in groundbreaking inventions rather than building organizations.

As the century rolled on, our interest and curiosity were piqued by those who moved smoothly between the world of business and the glamour of Hollywood (Howard Hughes) or—even better—business, Hollywood, *and* politics (Joseph Kennedy). In the early years of the television era business builders as different in demeanor and taste as Walt Disney and Hugh Hefner managed to become media personalities. Later occasional folk heroes like Lee Iacocca and H. Ross Perot emerged—the kind of businessmen who talked like workingmen.

Most Americans then and now have probably never heard of managerial genius Alfred Sloan (General Motors). But their attentions were captured and imaginations sparked when corporate warrior Ralph Nader stood up to the mighty GM in the mid-1960s—just as Erin Brockovich did against Pacific Gas & Electric in the 1990s.

Of course the media generally and Hollywood in particular played a key role in amplifying and dramatizing these battles, passing out the black hats and the white hats to the various players according to the studio magnates' own ideologies and their sense of what would sell. During the 1980s, for example, Hollywood executives (no shrinking violets themselves when it comes to hard-nosed business practices) found in the executive suite fodder for some of popular entertainment's most memorable villains, such as J. R. Ewing and Gordon Gecko. It continues to irk many in the business community that Hollywood almost invariably depicts businesspeople as the bad guys in movies and television. Indeed, one survey revealed that businesspeople in prime time television are three times more likely to commit murder, theft, and drug deals than the criminals depicted in the same shows!

Yet over the last 10 to 15 years, the explosion of new media outlets such as cable television and the Internet, as well as the entry of tens of millions of middle-class professionals into equity markets, has helped heighten interest in business and business leaders. Viewers can now invite some of those "boring, balding blue-suited businessmen" right into their living rooms and offices to find out how their family nest eggs are doing and how to emulate those business success stories and grow rich.

With the introduction of life-altering technologies, a new media spotlight has also been turned on a new breed of business leaders like Steve Jobs and Bill Gates. And, as executive suites have diversified, content-hungry media outlets are readily available to document the change, highlighting women business leaders like Hewlett-Packard CEO Carly Fiorina.

Finally, business has also benefited from a relative decline in the stature of more traditional sources of leadership such as politics. With the end of the cold war and the arrival of sustained prosperity in the 1990s, the decisions made in the political arena somehow don't seem as momentous. The questionable conduct and ethics of the political class has accelerated its decline as a source of heroes and role models as well. Taking all these developments into account, reflect on this question: During the 1990s who really had a greater impact on your life and society—Bill Clinton or Bill Gates?

BUSINESS LEADERSHIP: THE RECORD

THIS FRESH LOOK at the business leadership of our nation is long overdue. If Americans would fully consider the business track record over the past century they might better understand what the business giants of that time, up to and including today, have to offer.

All one has to do is contrast what life was like in the year 1900 with what it was like in the year 2000 to understand the change, growth, and progress achieved by Americans during the hundred years in between.

In 1900:

- America was home to 76 million people. Life expectancy was just 48 years.

- America's workforce totaled 29 million. Just under 19 percent of women participated in that workforce. Over a third—37.5 percent—of working Americans toiled on farms.

- Less than 13 percent of adults were high school graduates—just 3 percent had college degrees. Only 1,965 graduate degrees were awarded in the entire nation. Women earned just 20 percent of college degrees.

- Just 1 percent of Americans owned stock.

By 2000:

- America was home to 283 million people. Life expectancy reached 78 years.

- The workforce totaled 137.7 million. Nearly 60 percent of women participated. Some 98 million Americans worked in service industries, while just 1.6 percent worked on farms.

- Over 80 percent of adults were high school graduates and 24 percent earned college degrees. Women earned more than 50 percent of these degrees. Over 500,000 graduate degrees were awarded nationwide.

- Over half—52 percent—owned stock.

In their book *The First Measured Century,* scholars at the American Enterprise Institute (AEI) elaborate further on a century of remarkable economic and social progress:

- Output per person increased eight times over the course of the century.

- U.S. investment in the global economy grew 140 times over.

- The average income of middle-income households rose from $15,745 in 1929 to $47,809 in 1998—*after* adjusting for inflation.

- The poverty rate declined from 22 percent in 1959 to 12 percent in 1999.

- American business revenues grew from $2 trillion in 1939 to $18 trillion in 1996.

- Stock exchange volume multiplied 3,000 times between 1900 and 1999.

Together these and other developments added up to a life of enviable quality and leisure in 2000 compared to 1900. In the words of AEI: "The amount of time Americans spent working declined dramatically. The workday declined from ten hours to eight hours. The six-day workweek became a five-day workweek. Americans entered the labor force at older ages because of increased formal schooling. They left the labor force at earlier ages because of retirement. Among men aged sixty-five and over, 63 percent worked in 1900 but only 17 percent worked in 2000."[3]

Economist Stanley Lebergott dramatizes the improvements in the American lifestyle—particularly for women—even more vividly in his book *Pursuing Happiness: American Consumers in the 20th Century:* "In 1900, cooking, baking, food preserving, and canning were nearly all done at home. Most clothing was made, washed, and repaired at home. Not to mention house cleaning, childcare, and medicating the sick. Since families took less than two days of vacation a year, virtually all recreation was likewise produced at home."

Lebergott goes on to estimate that the typical housewife circa 1900 carried seven tons of coal, hauled 9,000 gallons of water, and baked a half a ton of bread per year![4]

THE BUSINESS ROLE
IN AMERICA'S PROGRESS

WHAT EXPLAINS THIS CENTURY of progress in the abundance, quality, and length of American life?

Was it the fact that the nation has been blessed by geography—populating a vast continent rich in natural resources and separated from prior centuries of turmoil by two vast oceans? Yes.

Was it the fact that American society has been continually renewed and revitalized by succeeding waves of immigrants who brought their energies, talents, and dreams to our shores? Yes.

Was it because of a democratic political system and form of government that protects the aspirations of individuals from the plunder and tyranny of kings and dictators? Yes.

Have we been blessed with more than our share of brilliant scientists, inventors, doctors, and medical researchers whose developments and breakthroughs made us more productive, comfortable, and healthy? Yes.

And have we been honored by millions of brave men and women who have repeatedly put their lives on the line defending America and its promise from enemies seeking to conquer or destroy us? Absolutely.

Each of these blessings contributed strongly to the greatest and most prosperous nation on earth. But underlying it all has been a free enterprise system that—while far from perfect—has generated the growth, wealth, and opportunity to make all other advances possible. The business and entrepreneurial leaders brought to the fore by that system have been indispensable to its success.

One of the most misunderstood—or conveniently ignored—truisms of our age is that economic growth, fueled by the promise of wealth and profits, is perpetually in conflict with gentler values such as a clean environment, support for the arts, the aspirations of workers, or a social safety net for the poor.

In fact it is economic growth that pays the bills for such virtuous pursuits. Travel anywhere in the world and you will quickly see that the least developed economies have the dirtiest environments, the greatest levels of human squalor, and the harshest, most punishing lifestyles for average people. And in almost every case the countries in the worst shape with the least progress for everyday citizens have been those with the greatest level of government control and central planning over the economic decisions of the people.

During the 20th century, the lead players in the American economic miracle and the nation's success have been the men and women of business—from the chief executives of big companies like Jack Welch to the small-town entrepreneurs to the dreamers and contrarians who have constantly challenged business to do better.

The Evolving Bottom Line

The business community can point to another set of less orthodox achievements over the past century, achievements that have greatly enhanced its leadership role in society.

Few would dispute that the principal goal of any business is and must be to make a profit. For the small business owner, that profit constitutes a livelihood—the money that's left to support a family when all the bills are paid. For the large corporation, the profits that aren't plowed back into business expansion are returned to investors in the form of dividends. Increasingly, these investors include millions of Main Street Americans whose pensions depend on the growth and income from stocks in the country's largest companies. Yet even though the business community continued to focus on profit over the course of the 20th century, it also developed a strong social conscience and commitment to the community, producing tremendous contributions that have enriched the lives of all Americans.

Some would argue that business not only had to be pushed to show concern for the plight of workers, the condition of the environment, or the social conditions of the community—it had to be shoved! The more realistic assessment is that attitudes on these issues evolved in the business community as they evolved in society as a whole. Most businesspeople adopted a larger view of their role in society, believing that by enriching the entire community they were not only doing the right thing but in fact helping improve the overall business environment and thus their company and its profit potential. This makes the case for looking to business for positive leadership role models all the more compelling.

When evaluating society's progress in the 20th century and the business role in that progress, one critical point must be underscored: Without a strong economy and broad-based prosperity produced by American business, little if any gains in working conditions, environmental quality, equality of opportunity, health care, or education and the arts would be possible. A strong, productive economy is what pays the bills for all these worthy goals and compelling missions.

It is time to start recognizing the key players behind this success and give them pedestals of at least the height and breadth of those we provide for our leaders in sports, politics, and war.

A Gallery of Business Greats

The American business landscape, past and present, is populated with interesting, unlikely, and heroic figures—leaders with visions and also with flaws—whose lives offer many lessons about personal leadership in business and life. Most of us just never took the time or had the opportunity to get to know them! Here are just a few of the business builders, visionaries, and revolutionaries who belong on any list of outstanding leaders of the last 100 years:

Douglas Boeing (1881–1956) began by building and flying seaplanes in the earliest days of flight. Douglas Boeing then laid the foundation for a company that has outlasted all domestic competitors and still reigns supreme over global aviation.

Walt Disney (1901–1966) was taking a train trip between New York and Los Angeles when the vision of a funny mouse, later named Mickey, popped into his head. From the creation of that mouse came an entertainment giant that today is valued at $20 billion and whose products are known around the world.

Henry Ford (1863–1946) put the horseless carriage within reach of average families and thus created America's car culture. More than that, he revolutionized manufacturing with his assembly line methods and was one of the first industry titans to understand the link between happy, satisfied workers and productivity.

William Henry Gates III (1955–) ushered in the Internet age. This Harvard dropout created the language and the easy-to-use programs that turned computer hardware into the most powerful set of tools ever placed in human hands.

Amadeo Giannini (1870–1949) gave us consumer banking as we know it today. Giannini devised the first system of bank branches, emphasizing convenience for customers, and his Bank of America pioneered and popularized installment loans to individuals, which today drive so much of our consumer economy.

William Hewlett (1913–2001) and *David Packard* (1912–1996) started their company in a garage with an investment of about $500. Beginning with sound-testing equipment and later moving into computers, Hewlett and Packard built a global powerhouse years before anyone had heard of Silicon Valley or the PC.

Lee Iacocca (1924–) oversaw the development and marketing of the Mustang at Ford. At Chrysler he engineered the company's bold comeback in the 1980s. Beyond that he pioneered the concept of the businessman as just an average guy on the street, winning white-collar and blue-collar fans alike with his pithy comments about economic and trade issues.

Ray Kroc (1902–1984) was already 52 when he saw the crowd of people pulling into the McDonald brothers' hamburger stand in San Bernadino, California. Ray Kroc surmised that the busy, young, and mobile families of the post–World War II years wanted drive-in restaurants that were fast, familiar, and consistent in quality and price. Thus the fast food industry as we know it today was born.

William Levitt (1897–1994) did more than any other single person to create suburban America. His Levittown subdivision in New York offered affordable detached homes in a planned community for the growing middle class—and the concept rapidly spread across the country.

Akio Morita (1921–1999) almost single-handedly changed the image of Japanese-made products in the United States and around the world—from cheap schlock to the highest quality. Morita and his Sony Corporation also triggered a consumer electronics revolution by making affordable but reliable products available to the mass market and by offering innovations like the Sony Walkman.

Robert N. Noyce (1927–1990) developed an efficient method of connecting transistors and other electronic components into a single integrated circuit and later founded Intel. Today, Intel's most sophisticated microprocessor contains some 9.5 million transistors in a single chip.

H. Ross Perot (1930–) made his fortune by building Electronic Data Systems (EDS) but became a household name through his adventures in politics and international derring-do. He staged a successful mission to free employees held in the Ayatollah's Iran. In the 1992 presidential election he garnered 19 million votes as an independent candidate.

William Shockley (1910–1989) and his team of developers at Bell Labs orchestrated the first giant step into the age of technology by introducing the transistor in 1948. This device replaced the much larger and less reliable vacuum tube in electronic devices and spawned entire generations of new products and industries.

Alfred P. Sloan Jr. (1876–1966) not only built the General Motors behemoth but also created a corporate management system that was emulated for decades.

Frederick Smith (1944–) wrote a term paper at Yale arguing for an overnight delivery service that would meet the needs of a just-in-time economy and fill the service gaps left by the U.S. postal monopoly. While he earned only a C grade on the paper, Smith soon translated its ideas into Federal Express, which today delivers packages to more than 200 countries in 600 aircraft and 46,000 trucks.

Ted Turner (1938–) popularized the concept of cable superstations that broadcast programming all over the nation. By creating CNN he challenged the news dominance of the three major networks and filled an increasing demand for 24-hour news.

Jay Van Andel (1925–) and *Rich deVos* (1926–) created Amway—the direct selling giant that markets consumer products and services in a network marketing system. Some 30 million people worldwide have joined Amway and other companies like it, taking advantage of a low-cost business opportunity and building their own direct selling organizations.

Sam Walton (1918–1992) invented the modern retailing system, opening huge stores offering discount prices in suburbs and rural areas that became economic anchors in those communities. The seeds planted by this Arkansas businessman have today grown into Wal-Mart, the second-largest company in America.

Harry Warner (1881–1958) and *Jack Warner* (1892–1978) released *The Jazz Singer* in 1927—the first movie with a sound track synchronized to the film images. This revolutionized the industry and ignited a Golden Age in Hollywood. Their efforts helped establish entertainment as a major 20th-century industry and America as its undisputed leader.

Thomas Watson (1914–1993) envisioned a great future in machines that tabulated data and from that idea and other innovations such as the electric typewriter, built IBM into a global giant and a much-respected symbol of American economic power and excellence.

Robert Woodruff (1889–1985) became president of a beverage company his father and a group of investors had purchased several years earlier. Woodruff quickly began to pioneer many of the marketing strategies that are still effective today. He relied heavily on market research, linked his product to a distinctive lifestyle, and ensured consistency in the product worldwide. In the process he made Coca-Cola one of the most widely recognized brands in human history.

Steve Wozniak (1950–) and *Steve Jobs* (1955–) rejected the assumptions that computers should be confined to business use and would always take up huge amounts of space and cost. Their vision, which they helped turn into reality through Apple, was to make the computer *personal* and place easy-to-use machines in the hands of average people. Their early efforts initiated the era of home computing.

Wilbur Wright (1867–1912) and *Orville Wright* (1871–1948) were better inventors than they were businessmen—and what an invention! By inventing and successfully flying the first airplane, the Wright brothers altered human beings' sense of time, space, and reality forever.

And Then There's Jack

The following pages establish—through examples, decisions, actions, statements, and the views of others—just why General Electric's Jack Welch has earned an undisputed place in this gallery of great business leaders. Here are some of the leadership lessons and ideas emerging from his life and career:

- You don't have to attend Ivy League schools or possess extraordinary innate skills and a rich family pedigree to become a great leader. Nor do you have to be six feet tall with movie-star looks and a velvety radio voice. *Ask Jack Welch! At 5'8" tall, and with a sharp Boston accent punctuated by a lifelong stutter, no one ever accused him of being "mediagenic."*

- A leader is a fierce competitor but picks each battle carefully—choosing battles that can be won. *That's why Welch gave up hockey and football for golf and for years insisted that GE only emphasize businesses where it could place first or second in the market.*

- On the big issues be ready to walk away from the safe and comfortable course in defense of your principles and to do what you think is right. *Jack Welch once handed in his resignation because of what he believed to be unfair treatment.*

- Change is something to embrace and take advantage of. But don't be so arrogant to think that you can steer its course or predict it long term. *None of the experts predicted the cataclysmic Asian financial crisis of 1997, not even Welch.*

- If it ain't broke, break it yourself and make it better. Change before you have to—and do it more than once. *Jack Welch confounded business experts when he changed a healthy GE in 1981. He did it again in the 1990s.*

- Keep your eyes fixed on reality and attuned to the changing environment around you. The strategy that made you a genius yesterday may transform you into a fool tomorrow. *That's one reason Jack Welch jettisoned his "number one–number two" business strategy after many years. It wasn't working anymore.*

- Be willing to buck the conventional wisdom—including your own. *Welch did so by constructing a hugely successful conglomerate when most of the experts were calling such companies dinosaurs.*

- Stand up lonely against the crowd but be willing to check and double-check your own premises. *Did Welch listen carefully enough to the preponderance of pundits who warned that his Honeywell deal would run into fierce resistance from European regulators?*

- Hate bureaucracy with a passion. Root it out—corner it and kill it. Winning organizations must shed excess process and emphasize speed and simplicity. *Jack Welch believes the Internet may represent the dagger in the heart of bureaucracy.*

- In place of bureaucracy build a meritocracy. Invest in and pay for success. Reward people according to performance. Take a personal interest in the best and get rid of the worst. *Welch quit GE once because he got the same raise as everyone else. His huge raises for stars and layoffs of unnecessary or underperforming employees are legendary.*

- A leader focuses on creating leaders, not followers. Surround yourself with strong people, people who will even challenge you but also those who not only perform but who embrace your organization's core values. *Welch insisted he would rid GE of top performers who failed to operate in a manner that embraced company values of openness and teamwork.*

- Information is *still* power. Share it. Empower your stars, improve speed and boost performance by ripping walls, boundaries, and layers from your organization. But understand that this is easier said than done. *Many CEOs claim and believe they run flat organizations but they really don't. Is Jack Welch one of them?*

- Have a vision and spread it around. People need to believe in something beyond their own paycheck and daily work routine. A manager signs checks and balances books. A leader crafts and communicates a compelling vision and a sense of mission. *Jack Welch's Six Sigma quality control program was one of many instances in which he rallied all levels of his vast organization behind a powerful idea.*

- Arguments bring people together. Engage in creative conflict where all members of your team are encouraged to contribute ideas, knock down old practices, and stand up to peers and superiors. *Welch's "Work-Out" program and sessions in "the Pit" at Crotonville instilled this culture at General Electric.*

- Live on the "lunatic fringe." Make bold moves and big decisions. *Jack Welch did this when he announced the purchase of RCA in 1985 and tried to buy Honeywell on the eve of his retirement.*

- A leader strives to work harder and with more intensity and commitment than anyone else in the organization. *Welch believed that managers who had to work 90 hours a week were doing something wrong, but there is no evidence that he did much of anything other than live and breathe for his company.*

- A leader is really a teacher, a trainer, and an idea generator. *Welch believed it was his duty to spend a majority of his time mentoring others and developing big ideas, as illustrated by his frequent visits to the GE management development center at Crotonville.*

- Have a global view—not only as you search for markets, but also for human talent, ideas, and better ways of doing things. *Welch's GE draws employee talent from all over the world and the company is close to deriving a majority of its revenues from international sources.*

- Stay on top of your game until the very end. Always be part of the change, not the establishment. If you feel your energy flagging, your courage waning, or your complacency rising—or your openness to new ideas shrinking—it's time to go. *This almost happened to Jack Welch with his early closed-mindedness to the Internet, but his nearly unprecedented 20-year reign as GE's chairman suggests durability and a continuous process of revitalization in his leadership.*

- Control your destiny—or someone else will. It's a familiar Welch credo and never more important when grooming and choosing the leaders who will take your place. *The process Welch employed to pick Jeffrey Immelt as the next chairman and CEO was skillful— but the jury will be out for some time as to whether this process produced a winner. Meanwhile, Welch will put his own stamp on his GE record through post-retirement writings and speeches.*

Management expert Warren Bennis has said: "Good leaders make people feel that they're at the very heart of things, not at the periphery. Everyone feels that he or she makes a difference to the success of the organization. When that happens, people feel centered and that gives their life meaning."[5]

Jack Welch's focus was always people—and that meant the "tough love" of layoffs and critical performance reviews as well as the softer values of empowerment and inclusion. It's this focus that makes his ideas and approaches so accessible and applicable for the vast majority who will never run giant corporate conglomerates but who seek to inspire others and successfully move organizations, companies, small enterprises, employees, and fellow citizens in positive directions.

CHAPTER 2

JACK WELCH'S "EARNINGS AND CASH ENGINE"

Edison would be pleased.
—JACK WELCH ASSESSING GE
AT THE END OF THE 20TH CENTURY

GENERAL ELECTRIC calls itself "a diversified services, technology and manufacturing company." Jack Welch has called it "an accelerating earnings and cash engine."

It is certainly that. In 20 years under Welch's leadership, a company many doubted could be improved upon at all when he took over became the most admired large company in the world. In GE investors found the ideal combination of impressive growth in shareholder value and income alongside the security and stability of putting their money in an American institution governed by a business legend.

When Welch began his tenure at the top in April 1981, he found a company geared toward consumer products such as TVs, lighting, and appliances. Annual revenues were $28 billion, generated mostly from domestic markets. Like most big corporations of that day, GE was laden with staff—some 440,000 people. Sales averaged just over $69,000 per employee. The company's market capitalization totaled $13 billion and its shares traded at about nine times earnings.[1]

Twenty years later, financial services constituted the company's most profitable group of businesses. Seventy percent of GE's revenues came from services, compared to 15 percent when Welch took over. The company no longer made televisions. It owned the oldest and most successful television network instead.

Annual revenues in 2000 reached nearly $130 billion, with more than 40 percent derived from promising foreign markets. General Electric operated in more than 100 countries and employed 313,000 people worldwide. Sales per employee averaged over $382,000.

GE stock was routinely described as "defying gravity," trading at roughly 40 times earnings. For the year 2000, the company ranked third in sales (after Exxon Mobil and Wal-Mart) and in profits (after Exxon Mobil and Citigroup), but first in the world in market value—besting some very tough competition, as evidenced by the most recent top ten list:

1. General Electric $486.67 billion ($498.64 billion by May 2001)

2. Microsoft $369.10 billion

3. Exxon Mobil $306.67 billion

4. Pfizer $270.80 billion

5. Citigroup $260.80 billion

6. Wal-Mart Stores $231.15 billion

7. AOL Time Warner $230.48 billion

8. Royal Dutch/Shell $216.50 billion

9. BP $199.79 billion

10. IBM $196.86 billion[2]

General Electric's 2.1 million shareowners fared well under Welch, realizing an average annual return of nearly 24 percent. This average was greatly surpassed in recent years. In 1997, 1998, and 1999 total return to GE shareholders reached 51 percent, 41 percent, and 54 percent respectively.

The stock split five times during his tenure, the last being a 3 for 1 split in April 2000. The quarterly dividend, reaching 16 cents per share, was paid and in fact increased every quarter after Welch became CEO. According to Janet Lowe, author of two books on Welch, a $10,000 investment in General Electric stock on the eve of his ascension to CEO would have been worth more than $640,000 by the end of 1999—assuming all dividends were reinvested in additional GE stock purchases.[3]

It was thus a well-satisfied Jack Welch who was able to report on the occasion of his final address to share owners as CEO that "2000 was our best year ever. Revenues were up 16 percent to nearly $130 billion. Net income was up 19 percent to $12.7 billion. Earnings per share up 19 percent."

And despite a weakening economy, Welch brashly predicted more of the same in 2001. "We'll deliver earnings growth at a time when many are delivering earnings warnings. Our first quarter results [for 2001] demonstrated this with earnings up 15 percent. We're confident GE will have another record year in 2001."[4]

Positive testimonials about Welch's performance began to pour in early and often—at least from business writers and publications. Just one year into his job, Welch saw his new leadership approach at the company heralded in the *Wall Street Journal,* which published an article headlined "New GE Chairman Wants Managers to Be Entrepreneurs" on July 12, 1982.[5] By 1984 the *Washington Post* was ready to declare "GE's Welch Powering Firm into Global Competitor." By the time he had spent six years on the job, he was regularly topping polls of businesspeople as the most admired business executive in America.[6]

By the mid-1990s accolades for Welch's GE became commonplace:

- Global Most Admired Company: *Fortune* (1998, 1999, 2000)

- World's Most Respected Company: *Financial Times* (1998, 1999, 2000)

- America's Most Admired Company: *Fortune* (1998, 1999, 2000, 2001)

- America's Greatest Wealth Creator: *Fortune* (1998, 1999, 2000)

- First: *Forbes* Super 100 (1998, 1999, 2000)

- First: *Business Week* 1000 (1999)

- First: *Business Week*'s 25 Best Boards of Directors (2000)

- "Manager of the Century": *Fortune* (1999)

As Welch's retirement loomed, the assessments of his performance became especially fulsome. "He is truly, truly one of the most extraordinary executives I have ever met," Gerry

Roche, a leading executive-recruitment expert told *Newsweek* in December 2000. "He has the extraordinarily rare combination of being a visionary, of being conceptual, of being very bright, and yet, of being very operational."[7]

"This guy's legacy will be to create more shareholder value on the face of the planet than ever—forever," gushed a Wall Street securities analyst to *Business Week* in 1998. In its own wrap-up review in 2001, the *Wall Street Journal* called Welch "a perpetual improvement machine." Canada's *National Post* told its readers that Welch is "regarded as one of the greatest CEOs of his time, perhaps one of the best CEOs of the 20th century." The *Economist* of London called him "the Princess Diana of the business press: he adorns covers because he sells them."[8]

Even after his eve-of-retirement deal to buy Honeywell fell victim to obstinate European regulators (see Chapter 5 for more details), some analysts sized the snafu up as little more than a blip. "His reputation of creating value for shareholders and making tough business decisions remains unbesmirched," stated the *New York Times.*[9]

Still, as Welch's reputation soared to stratospheric heights near the end of his GE reign, a countervailing strain of commentary began to appear. This was inevitable. As anyone in the political or entertainment worlds knows, the bigger the reputation the bigger the target for the born contrarians, the jealous also-rans, and the genuinely differing to shoot at. As Welch was fond of putting it: "The higher the monkey climbs, the more his ass is exposed."[10]

The centerpiece work of this critical, revisionist school of thought is former *Wall Street Journal* reporter Thomas O'Boyle's *At Any Cost,* which appeared in 1998. The book indicts General Electric under Welch for abandoning "the old-fashioned business values that made this the American century—loyalty, trust, respect, teamwork, hard work, compassion—in a feverish pursuit of the quick buck."

Welch himself is portrayed as not only ruthless and vain (standard portrayals of the corporate elite by antibusiness critics) but more surprisingly, as capricious and not altogether competent in his decision making. Even so, O'Boyle acknowledges, "That Welch has changed General Electric—and that shareholders have benefited enormously—is undeniable."[11]

In the end I don't share O'Boyle's view of Jack Welch and General Electric because I don't share his negative view of modern business and late-20th-century capitalism. The book is well written and researched, however. Unfair as it often is, it is challenging and thought-provoking.

Other critics have appeared more recently. A cover story in the June 18, 2001, *New Republic* is titled "Jack Welch, America's Most Overrated CEO." The article also acknowledges Welch's successes but claims that other companies have done better during the same period and that a sizable share of his larger-than-life reputation derives from aggressive public relations and artful management and release of earnings statements and other company developments.

Similarly, the *National Post* has charged: "In order to report steadily rising profits, GE sometimes offsets an extraordinary gain on the sale of an asset with extraordinary losses from a restructuring charge, and that way avoids reporting a profit so high that it cannot be topped in the next reporting period. It also times the sale of some equity stakes to generate profit gains where needed."[12]

The paper goes on to suggest that "managing" a company's income statement in this fashion is one of the lessons

Welch has taught the American business community. But Jack Welch didn't invent what is undoubtedly an overreliance on quarterly earnings reports by investors. He did, however, correctly foresee the intense competition for the investors' dollars that would arise out of a U.S. economy and equity marketplace that were undergoing deregulation, globalization, and a revolution in the application of information technologies. These changes meant that companies would have to make money, that management decisions would be transparent for all to view and critique, and that companies would have to continually make their case to shareholders in aggressive ways.

As for the notion that a superpowered PR machine was substantially responsible for Welch's reputation, there is no question that like any Fortune 100 CEO, he was aided by a stable of public relations polishers. But from my observation (backed by a 20-year career in communications), there was nothing out of the mainstream in terms of image promotion or management on the part of either Welch or GE. People just assume that it was happening because in a community where most CEOs suffer poor or nonexistent public perceptions, Jack Welch was and remains a standout.

Welch's achievements are real. So are his mistakes, of which there have been plenty. It is the extent by which the achievements outweigh the errors, along with Welch's unique ability to communicate the reasons and the values behind his actions and his aggressive but appealing personality—and the fact that he led a company the size of GE—that together explain his stature as a business leader.

And he has been amply rewarded for his efforts. In 2000, Welch's compensation totaled $122.5 million, comprising $16.7 million in salary and bonus along with $48.7 million in a restricted stock award and $57.1 million from exercised stock options. According to *Business Week,* the sum total made Welch the seventh-highest paid company chief (following two Citigroup executives and the CEOs of AOL Time Warner, Cisco Systems, Cedant, and Tyco International).[13]

There's little doubt Welch thinks he's worth every penny. During a blunt exchange with college students in early 2001 chronicled by the *Wall Street Journal,* the reporter noted, "The GE leader was asked about the disparity between executive salaries and the wages of workers toiling in the company's plants in Mexico. 'The last time I looked, no one came to GE with a gun to their head,' he responded. 'They went there because it was the best job they could find.' Why not offer stock options to all employees he was then asked? 'The dumbest idea in the world,' Welch answered. 'Stock options should be a reward system that reinforces genuine evaluations.'"[14]

THE GE PLATFORM

SO HOW DID Jack Welch do it?

To start with, he had a great company to work with—the resources and the reputation of one of America's best corporations, General Electric. It is hard to overstate the strength and breadth of the platform on which Jack Welch built his own record of achievement. Chances are if he had been running a manufacturing company in Atlanta or a retail firm in Minneapolis, most Americans would never have heard of Jack Welch regardless of his talents as a business leader. Then again if he had spent his career running a company like those, he wouldn't be Jack Welch!

The "house that Jack built" at General Electric was constructed on a monumental foundation. None other than Thomas Alva Edison laid the cornerstone. The inventor established the Edison Electric Company in 1878 in an effort to transform his invention of the incandescent lamp into a practical and commercial reality.

In 1889 various Edison operations were consolidated to form the Edison General Electric Company. Three years later that firm merged with the Thomson-Houston Electric Company and General Electric was born.

The newly formed company issued 100 shares of stock at an initial sales price of $100 per share. When the Dow Jones Industrial Average was devised in 1896, General Electric was on it. The company is the only corporation on the original list that is still there today. And suppose you were fortunate enough to have had an ancestor who purchased just one share of GE stock back in the company's earliest days? Assuming the stock was never sold and all dividends were plowed back into additional stock purchases, by the end of 2000 you'd have been the proud owner of 150,107 shares of GE stock, worth a cool $7.2 million.

Clearly, handsome returns for investors at General Electric did not begin with Jack Welch. Nor did the company's renowned reliability when it comes to paying dividends. GE has paid quarterly dividends without interruption since 1899. Those dividends have been increased each quarter since 1975.

A LEGACY OF SUCCESS AND INNOVATION

YET INVESTOR RETURN and reliability represent just one piece of the formidable business platform presented to Jack

Welch when he became CEO in 1981. The company's long history of innovation throughout the past century touched and enhanced virtually every aspect of modern life. Developments fostered by GE played a leading role in making the American lifestyle more convenient, enjoyable, mobile, and healthy. By the end of its first hundred years of operation (1978), for example, the company had become the first organization in history to register over 50,000 patents.

The following milestones are among those that illustrate the company's innovative prowess since its founding:

1879—Edison invents the carbon filament incandescent lamp. The first commercially practical lamp lasts for 40 hours.

1880—Further innovations by Edison extend his lamps' life to 600 hours. The first lamp factory is opened in Menlo Park, New Jersey.

1896—A GE engineer builds electrical equipment for the production of X-rays and demonstrates their use in diagnosing bone fractures.

1900—GE opens the first industry laboratory for scientific research, in Schenectady, New York.

1902—A GE consulting engineer patents the electric fan.

1903—GE installs the largest steam turbine yet developed, a 5,000-kilowatt unit in Chicago.

1905—GE's first electric toaster hits the market.

1906—The world's first radio broadcast is accomplished by a GE engineer after he developed the high-frequency alternator that made radio broadcasts possible.

1908—GE develops and supplies electric locomotives for the New York Central Railroad.

1910—GE makes the first Hotpoint electric range.

1912—GE builds the first electrically propelled U.S. Navy ship, the *Jupiter*.

1914—GE designs the electrically controlled locks for the Panama Canal.

1915—The safety of electric stoves is significantly enhanced with GE's development of a ceramic insulation called Calrod.

1918—GE develops a new alternator that makes possible the first transoceanic radio communication. Also, a new GE vacuum tube is invented that later becomes a key component in radar systems and microwave ovens.

1921—GE's Sanford Moss develops the supercharger that paves the way for high-speed, high-altitude airline flight.

1922—GE opens radio station WGY in Schenectady, one of the first to transmit regular broadcasts.

1927—GE inaugurates the first television reception in a home in Schenectady.

1929—GE installs a new power generator unit in Indiana with a capacity four times greater than current models.

1930—GE puts the first electric washing machine on the market. The company also establishes its plastics division.

1932—The GE Credit Corporation is created to finance consumer purchases of the company's growing array of home appliances.

1935—New high-powered lamps from GE make possible the first nighttime major league baseball game, in Cincinnati, Ohio.

1940—WRGB in Schenectady, owned by GE, becomes the first station to relay broadcasts from New York City, laying the groundwork for the first television network.

1941—GE builds America's first jet engine.

1943—GE engineers invent the first airplane autopilot device.

1945—GE introduces the first commercial use of radar.

1947—Hotpoint, a GE brand, markets the first cooking equipment for fast-food restaurants.

1955—GE develops the process for manufacturing man-made diamonds, setting the stage for a new generation of industrial tools and machinery.

1956—Newly developed GE engines power the Convair Skylark, the first commercially viable jet plane. The company also establishes its management-training center in Crotonville, New York.

1962—A GE scientist invents the solid state laser, paving the way for the development of such products as the compact disc player and the laser printer.

1978—GE builds the world's largest nuclear power plant, in Japan.

1981—The revolution in fiber-optic communications is spurred by GE components that make possible 25-mile-long fiber-optic strands.

1986—New U.S. car models are introduced that contain a record amount of GE plastics as a substitute material for many components. Meanwhile, the firm completes its purchase, announced a year earlier, of RCA—and with it, NBC.

1991—GE passes IBM as the most highly valued company in America.

1992—GE builds the Mars Observer for NASA.

1994—GE becomes the first Fortune 500 company outside the computer industry itself to go online.

1999—GE Medical Systems introduces a new imaging technology that allows doctors and surgeons the clearest picture yet of diseases within the human body.[15]

ALONG WITH SUCCESS
AND INNOVATIONS . . . MISTAKES

ALONGSIDE GE'S formidable record of financial performance, product innovation, and positive societal impact stands a series of mistakes, misconduct, and controversy. This is hardly surprising for an organization of as many as 440,000 people engaged in an array of diverse activities around the globe throughout a century of turmoil and change. These episodes occurred before and during Welch's reign as CEO. Unless successor Jeffrey Immelt designs a cure for human fallibility and temptation, they will go on happening long after Welch is gone.

Among the most notorious blunders, missteps, and controversies:

- The federal government sued General Electric more than a dozen times during the 1940s for antitrust violations.

- In the late 1950s the company was indicted for price fixing and other illegal market manipulations. Three GE executives went to prison.

- In 1985 GE was indicted on charges of defrauding the government on a defense contract. The company pleaded guilty to 108 counts.

- GE bought Wall Street brokerage house Kidder Peabody in 1986 and not only sank hundreds of millions of dollars into a bad investment but suffered scandal and embarrassment from a young bond trader's $350 million in phony profits from bogus trades.

- In 1988 the company was fined after it uncovered and reported bribes offered to the Egyptian military in an effort to win a contract.

- A similar incident afflicted GE's Aircraft Division in 1999. This time the recipient of monies was an Israeli general for steering an engine contract to the company.

- In 1994, GE faced charges that it had conspired with DeBeers of South Africa to fix diamond prices. A lawsuit resulted in the dismissal of the charges.

And there have been more complex problems as well:

PCBs: From the late 1940s to the mid-1970s, General Electric discharged more than a million pounds of toxic polychlorinated biphenyls (PCBs) into the Hudson River. GE and Jack Welch have resisted efforts to dredge the Hudson and remove a substance most believe contaminates fish, water, and soil and damages human health. The firm has sided with those who maintain that the PCBs are dissipating naturally over time and are better left undisturbed in their resting place.

Honeywell and other acquisitions: For various reasons a number of GE's business deals have not panned out or paid off. Critics like O'Boyle have attributed this to Welch's rashness, ego, and flawed business acumen. Given the sheer volume of acquisitions under Welch (over 100 each year for 1997–1999, for example), as well as the tumultuous economic environment of the 1980s and 1990s, the fact that some of these deals turned sour is not surprising. Given the undeniably solid performance of the company for many decades and especially during the 20 years of Welch's leadership, it is unfair and unfounded to bundle the "misfires" into a blanket indictment of GE or Welch.[16]

LEGACY OF LEADERS

WHEN JACK WELCH stepped into the corner office in Fairfield, Connecticut, in April 1981 he not only had more than a century-old legacy of invention and innovation to build on, he had a legacy of business leadership to learn from and live up to as well. In the annals of American business, Welch is not the first corporate legend to emerge from General Electric. The company had been led by other executives known, in varying degrees, for their vision, managerial creativity, public service, and longevity. Some like Welch spent their whole careers at GE, climbing from simple jobs to the highest post.

Here is the roll of GE's leaders:

Charles A. Coffin: President, 1892–1912; Chairman 1913–1922

Charles A. Coffin was General Electric's first president. Born in 1844, the Fairfield, Maine, native began his business career at his uncle's shoe company in Lynn, Massachusetts. He later established his own shoe manufacturing firm.

When the American Electric Co. of New Britain, Connecticut, founded by inventor Elihu Thomson, moved to the area, Coffin was recruited to lead it. The newly named Thomson-Houston Company went toe-to-toe with Thomas Edison's companies. In 1892 Edison's companies and Thomson-Houston merged, creating General Electric, with Coffin as its first chief executive officer.

While a fierce competitor, Coffin had a management style that was inclusive and empowering. He called employees *associates,* refrained from giving direct orders, and invited employee input. His mettle was greatly tested by the depression of 1893, which threatened to shut the company. His negotiations with J. P. Morgan resulted in a financial package that saved GE and put it on a course of rapid growth.

Coffin was a seminal leader in the early years of the burgeoning electric industry. He retired from the board chairmanship in 1922.

E. W. Rice: President, 1913–1922

Edwin W. Rice Jr. was a star pupil of Thomson-Houston founder Elihu Thomson, who was a professor at Philadelphia's Central High School. With Thomson, Rice played a leading role in developing many of the nation's first electrical products.

Moving from inventing to management, Rice became factory manager of Thomson-Houston's Lynn plant when he was just 22. In 1892 he was GE's first technical director and became vice president in charge of manufacturing and engineering in 1896. His most important contribution was the establishment of the GE Research Laboratory, a first for a U.S. industrial company.

In 1913 he succeeded Charles A. Coffin as president, while Coffin remained as chairman.

Gerard Swope: President, 1922–1940; 1942–1945

A proverbial Horatio Alger hero, Gerard Swope started out with the General Electric Company in 1893 as a laborer at $1 a day, landing a helper's job at GE's Chicago Service Shop during a visit to the World's Fair when he was 21. Less than 30 years later, in 1922 he became the company's third president.

He interrupted his early work with the company to finish a degree in electrical engineering at MIT. After graduating he began a career with Western Electric, moving up rapidly in the company's ranks and serving in wide-ranging business centers from New York to China.

It was GE's first president, Charles A. Coffin, who recruited Swope in 1919 and quickly assigned him the task of establishing the company's first international business. Swope became the first president of the newly formed International General Electric Company. In May 1922 he was named president of the entire company and served in that capacity for more than 20 years.

Charles E. Wilson: President, 1940–1942; 1945–1950

Charlie Wilson was born in New York City in 1886 to an English mother and an Irish father. After dropping out of school in the seventh grade, he took a job as an office boy and then a factory worker for a GE subsidiary. He attended night school while working. By the age of 21 he was plant superintendent. After a transfer to GE Appliances, Wilson's role expanded rapidly. In 1937, Wilson was elected executive vice president of General Electric. Two years later he succeeded Gerard Swope as president.

Wilson's tenure was interrupted by World War II. At the request of President Roosevelt, he became vice chairman of the War Production Board—with Swope coming out of retirement to fill the president's slot. After resuming his duties as GE chief, Wilson inaugurated a postwar growth era for GE, transforming it into a heavy industry company. In 1950 he left GE after 51 years upon being appointed by President Truman to direct the Office of Defense Mobilization.

Owen D. Young: Chairman, 1922–1940

Owen D. Young was born in 1874 on an upstate New York farm that his parents later mortgaged to send him to Boston University to study law. After his graduation in 1896, Young joined a prestigious Boston law firm, where he gained experience working for electrical engineering clients. This experience soon caught the eye of GE's president Charles A. Coffin, who named him chief counsel and vice president for policy at GE. One of his greatest contributions was the creation of the Radio Corporation of America in 1919, intended to rescue the nation's struggling radio industry. He served as chairman of RCA for 10 years.

In 1922 Young succeeded Coffin as chairman of GE, with Gerard Swope serving as president. He gained a major international reputation through his service on the German reparations commission in 1924. In 1929, Young was called upon to head another committee of experts to unify further German payments. Throughout the 1920s, Young was frequently mentioned as a possible Democratic candidate for president. He capped his wide-ranging career in the late 1940s by leading the commission that led to the creation of the state university system of New York.

Philip D. Reed: Chairman, 1940–1942; 1945–1958

Born in Milwaukee in 1899, Philip Reed attended the public schools there. After serving in World War I, he earned an electrical engineering degree from the University of Wisconsin. Turning down an initial job offer from GE, Reed instead moved to New York to study law. In 1926, GE beckoned again and this time the freshly minted lawyer-engineer took a post in the office of a company vice president.

Reed soon caught the attention of the company's leaders, Gerard Swope and Owen Young, who moved him quickly through the ranks and assigned him to a variety of special projects. In December 1937, he was appointed assistant to the president and two years later was elected chairman of the company.

World War II brought major assignments. Reed was named chief of the Bureau of Industries, War Production Board. In 1943, he headed the newly created U.S. Mission for Economic Affairs in London. He resumed his work with GE in 1945, serving another 13 years as chairman. He retired from GE in 1959 after 32 years of service.

Ralph J. Cordiner: Chairman and CEO, 1958–1963; President 1950–1958

Born in 1900 on a small farm in Walla Walla, Washington, Ralph J. Cordiner worked his way through college and joined the Edison General Electric Appliance Company, a GE affiliate, in 1923. After rapid advances on the West Coast, in 1932 he was transferred to Bridgeport, Connecticut, spearheading the growth of the company's appliance business.

In 1939 Cordiner left GE to become president of Schick, where he was widely credited with revitalizing that company. A wartime assignment on the War Production Board brought him in contact with GE president Charlie Wilson, who brought Cordiner back to GE in 1943.

In 1950, he was elected to the presidency, succeeding Wilson. Cordiner was elected chairman and CEO in 1958. He was known for his pioneering management approaches, especially the idea of decentralization that he saw as essential for large post–World War II corporations. He also established the GE Management Development Institute at Crotonville, New York, which later played a major role in Jack Welch's leadership approach at the company.

Gerald L. Phillippe: Chairman, 1963–1967; President, 1961–1963

Gerald "Flip" Phillippe rose through the ranks of GE in the Statistics Division, where he gained recognition for his managerial skills. In 1953 he was elected chief financial officer of the company. He served in this position until his election as president in 1961. He became chairman in 1963, succeeding Ralph Cordiner. Public service included a leadership role in establishing the Urban Coalition to fight poverty and strife. His untimely death in 1968 at the age of 59 cut short his opportunity to lead GE.

Fred J. Borch: Chairman and CEO, 1967–1972; President and CEO, 1963–1967

Fred Borch was born in 1910 in Brooklyn, New York, where his father was an electrical engineer. Summer jobs while a student at Case Western Reserve University included work on a construction project for an electric power transmission line. After graduating in 1931 he worked as an auditor with General Electric in the Lamp Division. He moved ahead in that division quickly. In 1953, he was asked to restructure the Lamp Division. An appointment in 1954 as vice president for Marketing Services brought him into close contact with then-CEO Ralph I. Cordiner, the man he succeeded as chief executive of General Electric. Subsequent promotions included group executive for the Consumer Products Group and executive vice president.

Borch was elected president and CEO of General Electric in 1963, and chairman in 1968. During his tenure, Borch engineered the start of the long era of growth that continued and accelerated during the Jack Welch era. Between 1963 and 1972 sales and earnings doubled.

Reginald H. Jones: Chairman and CEO, 1972–1981

Reg Jones spent his entire career with General Electric, beginning in 1939 in the company's Business Training Course. He worked in a broad range of the company's businesses, which paved the way for his appointment as chief financial officer in 1968 and senior vice president in 1970. In 1972 he became president, then chairman and CEO.

Known for his decency and statesmanlike demeanor, Jones commanded respect and was well liked by employees and the broader business community. He emphasized R&D and strategic planning, which even in the difficult years of the 1970s created substantial corporate growth. During Jones's tenure sales more than doubled and earnings nearly tripled.

He played an active public service role, serving as the head of the President's Export Council and the Business Roundtable. Like other GE leaders before and after, Jones spent a major portion of his time cultivating the company's future leaders. His most noteworthy protégé was, of course, Jack Welch.

JACK WELCH'S SEVEN WINNING WAYS

JACK WELCH HAD a hard act to follow, but he also had a great legacy to build upon and an unrivaled business platform from which to make bold moves and expose his leadership ideas to the business world and beyond. Looking at his business strategy through 20 years as GE leader, it's clear that Welch both followed in the footsteps of his predecessors and blazed new trails for the company.

The successful Welch business strategy at GE can be attributed to seven key approaches. Though describing them doesn't capture the totality of the Welch management or leadership philosophy, it does represent the seven "winning ways" he employed to turn a strong company into a phenomenally successful company.

Welch instituted an aggressive program of buying and selling. Businesses were acquired and discarded based on the changing realities of consumer tastes, the economic and political environment, and the relative strength of the competition. Welch entered markets where he could win, and got out of those where he couldn't win or where the prize was shrinking (such as nuclear power and defense). According to longtime Welch-watcher Janet Lowe, during his tenure as CEO he sold 350 businesses for a total of $23.8 billion—while acquiring some 900 businesses worth $105.8 billion.[17]

Welch squeezed excessive cost and cut corporate fat through restructuring and downsizing. He was a leader in the painful but necessary process that corporate America had to go through in the 1980s to survive in a fiercely competitive global economy. During his first 12 years as GE leader, he reduced the employee base of the company from some 440,000 to just over 200,000 (then building it again to 313,000). The cuts earned him the moniker "Neutron Jack"—from the bomb designed to kill people but leave buildings intact. Nevertheless, the private sector's restructuring moves of the 1980s, led by Welch, set the stage for the longest period of economic expansion in America's history, which filled the 1990s.

Welch turned General Electric into a post-industrial company where manufacturing, while still vital, took a back seat to services. Though reports of the demise of America's manufacturing base are misguided, the transition to a services and information economy is undeniable and explains much of the country's global economic leadership. Welch decided early on to make GE a part of this services and information economy rather than consign it to the shrinking manufacturing sector. He built a company that drew 70 percent of its revenues from services.

Welch placed an intense focus on shareholder value, product quality, and customer service. By fostering this culture he attracted record investment to GE even during economic downturns and in a fiercely competitive environment. Through initiatives such as the Six Sigma program, GE was able to avoid the reputation for shoddy products and poor service that afflicted many U.S. companies. Some critics believe Welch's obsession with earnings reports and stock prices—one that spread throughout corporate America—prompted business to callously cut employees and close plants, while also hurting its ability to implement long-term investments and visions. Welch's response: "A proper balance between shareholders, employees and communities is what we all strive to achieve. But it is a tough balancing act because, in the end, if you don't satisfy shareholders, you don't have the flexibility to do the things you have to do to take care of employees or communities. In our society, like it or not, we have to satisfy shareholders."[18]

Welch transformed GE into a truly global company. While General Electric had pursued overseas markets for some 80 years, Welch accelerated the company's integration into the rapidly globalizing economy of the 1980s and 1990s, taking the share of revenues generated from global operations from less than 20 percent to well over 40 percent during his tenure as CEO. With 95 percent of the world's population living outside U.S. borders, many of them in exploding markets like China, Welch's emphasis on globalization has been well-placed.

Welch embraced a culture of change and spread it throughout General Electric, making the company more nimble and less bureaucratic while others like it slid toward extinction. From getting rid of businesses (even those with high sentimental value like housewares) to buying NBC and embracing the Internet, Welch proved that his continual talk of GE's "love of change" was more than sloganeering. Maintaining "the soul of a small company in the body of a big company" proved to be an effective success formula during an era of tumultuous change.

Welch created a company that became a magnet for human talent, empowered that talent and transformed employ-

ees into leaders and committed stakeholders in GE success. There's hardly a CEO in America who doesn't claim that people are the company's most valuable asset. Through relentless efforts that he asserted consumed more than 50 percent of his time, Welch put meat on the bones of this corporate cliché. Training, mentoring, freewheeling exchanges, and a carefully calibrated system of carrots and sticks to spur peak performance significantly boosted company productivity and competitiveness. Equally important, these efforts—along with Welch's passionate leadership—made GE a place where people wanted to be, a place where things were happening, a place where people's hunger to be a part of a cause beyond themselves could be well nourished.

MAKING SENSE OF GENERAL ELECTRIC TODAY

WHAT EXACTLY IS General Electric today? A manufacturing company or a services firm? A communications company or a transportation company? A medical research firm or a developer and manufacturer of consumer products and industrial components? Is it a brick-and-mortar relic of the Old Economy or a leading e-business in the New Economy?

The answer is . . . yes. All of the above and then some. A review of General Electric's key businesses would surprise many Americans, whose image of the old electric light bulb company may be frozen somewhere in the hazy past.

Aircraft Engines: GE is the world's largest producer of large and small jet engines for commercial and military aircraft. The company and its partners claim more than 50 percent of the global market for large commercial jet engines.

Appliances: GE's brands include Monogram, Profile Performance, Profile, GE, and Hotpoint, which sell a broad range of refrigerators and freezers, ovens and ranges, washers and dryers, dishwashers, and room air conditioners.

Aviation Services: GE also operates one of the world's largest aircraft leasing companies, with a fleet of 850 aircraft.

Commercial Equipment Financing: GE provides smaller companies with a wide variety of lease, loan, and sale-leaseback plans to help them acquire and continually modernize business equipment.

Commercial Finance: Created in 1994, this GE business helps certain classes of companies finance their business activities.

Employers Reinsurance Corporation (ERC): This world-leading business provides risk transfer to insurance companies, Fortune 1000 companies, and health care providers.

Financial Assurance: This GE business comprises nine investment and insurance units to help consumers invest, manage, and grow their wealth.

GE Equity: This subsidiary of GE Capital—made up of 120 investment professionals, five business units, and a portfolio of over 150 companies—offers innovative deal structuring along with technology support, business training, portfolio company networking, and sourcing discounts.

Global Consumer Finance: This GE business provides credit services to leading retailers, auto dealers, and consumers in 29 countries around the world.

Industrial Systems: GE is a leading supplier of products used to distribute, protect, operate, and control electrical power. Circuit breakers, switches, transformers, switchboards, switchgear, meters, relays, and AC and DC electric motors are just some Industrial Systems products.

Lighting: GE remains a leading supplier of lighting products including incandescent, fluorescent, high-intensity discharge, halogen, and holiday lamps.

Medical Systems: The business that Welch successor Jeffrey Immelt ran prior to his selection, GE Medical Systems is a global leader in medical diagnostic imaging technology and services. Products include CT scanners, X-ray equipment, nuclear medicine cameras, and mammography systems. It manufactures, sells, and services these products in more than 100 countries.

Mortgage Insurance Corporation: This GE business provides private mortgage insurance to enable would-be homeowners to finance their houses.

NBC: The nation's first broadcast network, NBC also owns 13 television stations and operates MSNBC with Microsoft. Other holdings include CNBC, CNBC Europe, and CNBC Asia.

Plastics: This GE business was Jack Welch's training and proving ground before he became CEO. It makes plastics used in the computer, electronics, data storage, office equipment, automotive, building and construction, and other industries.

Power Systems: This GE business designs, manufactures, and services gas, steam, and hydroelectric turbines and generators for power production, pipelines, and industry in 119 countries around the world.

Real Estate: This unit finances and invests in a broad range of commercial and residential properties. Its loans range from $2 million for single-property mortgages to hundreds of millions for multi-property portfolios.

Specialty Materials: This outfit makes high-performance materials used in the computer, electronics, mining, automotive, construction, and other industries. Its most noteworthy products include GE Silicones, GE Superabrasives, GE Specialty Chemicals, and GE Quartz.

Structured Finance Group: This GE business is an equity investor and provider of financing and other services in commercial, industrial, energy, telecommunications, and transportation sectors. In the past five years, Structured Finance Group has financed over 200 transactions in excess of $8 billion and has assets of over $11 billion.

Transportation Systems: This heavyweight business makes more than half of the diesel freight locomotives in North America. Other products include passenger locomotives, engines for ships and large land vehicles, and advanced railway signaling and control systems.

Vendor Financial Services: This GE business offers financial services to equipment manufacturers, distributors, dealers, and end users.

As GE worked its way into the 21st century, some critics contended that the company's commitment to scientific invention and product innovation were dulled—that under Welch it focused more on buying and selling businesses than on the revolutionary developments that marked its history. It's also said that the dizzying array of seemingly unrelated businesses on a roster that has changed continuously reveals a company without a strong business mission.

Would Edison be pleased as Jack Welch has proclaimed? The inventor in fact was known to be disappointed that the firm established as the result of the merger between his company and Thomson-Houston no longer bore his name. While maintaining a business relationship with GE, he reportedly attended only one board meeting of the new General Electric. So whatever disappointment Edison may have felt over the course of his original company, he felt it early on. No doubt Edison would be astonished by the mostly positive impact GE has had on so many facets of modern life.

GE proponents point to the $2.2 billion in annual research and development expenditures as evidence of its continuing commitment to innovation. One could further argue that since its earliest days, the company has encompassed a diverse complement of businesses. After all, how much did toasters ever have in common with jet engines—or plastics with nuclear power plants?

As for out-of-the-box Welch moves like the purchase of RCA (and NBC) in 1986, can that not be seen as a return to the company's roots, given its historic role in both the science and content of radio and television broadcasting during the pioneering years of the 1920s and 1930s?

Welch always understood that his GE business plan defied simple or standard definition. He thought hard and talked often about how to answer the question, "What is General Electric today?" As he put it, GE is and must be a company governed by both "timely initiatives" and "timeless values." In his 1999 letter to shareholders, released in the spring of 2000, Welch elaborated:

"Much has been said of the difficulty of 'understanding' GE because of the enormous diversity of its products and services and the breadth of its global operations. But it's actually easy to understand this Company . . . if you look at the array of world-class businesses and grasp the two fundamental forces that drive GE—its social architecture and its operating system."[19]

Welch went on to describe his company's social architecture as the processes he instituted to fully engage every employee in the company—and encourage them to contribute ideas, suggest improvements, and register criticisms regardless of their job or rank. One technique for achieving this is called "Work-Out"—an ongoing series of thousands of sessions geared to improving products, eliminating waste and making the company more efficient.

The other technique is the cultivation of what Welch calls a "boundaryless" culture, where lines of stratification and bastions of bureaucracy are jettisoned in favor of information sharing and teamwork, with speed and simplicity the hoped-for results.

"The combination of involving everyone in the game and responding to this flow of ideas and information turned GE into what we are today—a learning company," Welch maintained.

Alongside this social architecture was the operating system of GE, developed, Welch said, "to channel and focus this torrent of ideas and put it to use through the medium of Company-wide 'initiatives.'" Since Welch believes institutions must always be "timely," these initiatives evolved over time. During his last months as GE chief, Welch appeared most enthused about programs to continue the company's transformation to a global and e-commerce firm. Through the Six Sigma quality program and product services initiatives, he attempted to increase GE's focus on improving customer productivity through customized, ongoing upgrades of GE's technologies and product configurations.

The elements of both the social architecture and operating system Welch created will be explored in further detail in subsequent chapters. Together they comprise a considerable portion of Welch's legacy as a leader. They were instrumental in helping him fulfill one of a leader's fundamental responsibilities—defining a mission and rallying people to that mission by offering them a system of beliefs and approaches that lift the spirits beyond the banality of daily work and life.

Indeed, they created a people-oriented culture at General Electric and lifted the sights of a great company considerably higher than that of either a "diversified services, technology and manufacturing company" or an "earnings and cash engine."

CHAPTER 3

THE UNLIKELY LEADER

———◆———

In the simplest terms, a leader is one who knows
where he wants to go, then gets up and goes.
—JOHN ERSKINE

H IS FATHER WORKED for the Boston & Maine railroad. His mother was a devout Catholic who wanted him to become either a priest or a doctor. He grew up in an average, lower-middle-class neighborhood in Salem, Massachusetts.

He loved sports, especially sandlot baseball and varsity hockey, but was an athlete of average skills. It wasn't a lack of practice and certainly not a shortage of competitiveness—it was his stature. His adult height never made it past 5'8".

He wasn't smooth, glib, or slick in demeanor. Practiced, polished charm could not be called upon to compensate for other shortcomings. A scrappy, rough-around-the-edges personality, a lifelong stutter, and a sharp Boston accent made sure of that.

None of it mattered. Jack Welch beat the law of averages to become an extraordinary leader in spite of it all. How? Why? Some clues show up in his response to a reporter who asked what he thought about the general appraisal that he and Alfred Sloan (the late chief of General Motors) were the two greatest corporate executives of the 20th century.

"I didn't know Alfred Sloan," was Welch's reply.[1]

SIMPLE BEGINNINGS

JOHN FRANCIS WELCH JUNIOR was born on November 19, 1935, to Grace and John Francis Welch. His parents had been trying for many years to have a baby, and Jack, who finally came along when his mother was 40, was an only child.

Welch's father worked as a railway conductor while his mother stayed at home. The Welch family was of decidedly modest means, but not impoverished. Nonetheless, Welch's upbringing was rich in other ways—especially in the presence of his beloved and incalculably influential mother.

His father's work kept him away from home from five in the morning until after seven in the evening most days. This, along with Welch Senior's somewhat withdrawn personality, meant that it was young Jack's strong-willed mother who became the most important person in his life. Welch's love for her was so strong and his respect for her abilities as a teacher and mentor so deep that he has found it hard to put into words.

"It was my mother who trained me, taught me the facts of life," Welch explains. "She wanted me to be independent. Control your own destiny—she always had that idea. Saw reality. No mincing words. . . . Always constructive. Always uplifting. And I was just nuts about her."

"Don't get me started on my mother. She's my whole game."[2]

Grace Welch's guidance was particularly critical in helping Jack deal with his stutter. "She told me I didn't have a speech impediment," Welch has recalled. "Just that my brain worked too fast."[3] Still, despite his reverence for his mother, he never did fulfill her dreams for his future. Instead of religious or medical studies, he chose chemistry and business.

Grace Welch died in 1966. Jack Welch later said that the fact she didn't live to see him rise at General Electric and become its chairman was the single biggest disappointment of his life.

A strong mother pumping her son full of self-confidence and the values of hard work and discipline—and perhaps the need to compensate for the insecurity that often afflicts those with speech impediments—turned the young Jack Welch into a dynamo at school, in sports, and later in business. Even though his innate athletic abilities were not much better than average, he was a fierce and combative competitor in baseball and basketball games at the Pit, an abandoned quarry in Salem, and later on the varsity hockey team at Salem High. Throughout his business career Welch would credit these experiences with honing his leadership skills, far more than what he learned in classrooms or boardrooms.

Nonetheless, teachers figured strongly in his life and no doubt influenced the focus he placed on training and mentoring at General Electric. The "leader as coach and teacher" concept—one of Welch's core management principles—sprang directly from his own positive experiences in sports and in school.

In school and throughout his career, Welch's athletic combativeness were matched by his verbal combativeness. A boyhood friend has recalled: "He was a nice, regular guy, but always very competitive, relentless and argumentative."[4] That view was not an isolated one. His high school classmates voted him the "most talkative and noisiest boy."

FIRST IN COLLEGE

JACK WELCH'S GRADES in high school were good enough to earn him a nomination for the ROTC scholarship he needed to pay for an Ivy League school. He didn't get it. Welch attributed the rejection to his family's lack of political connections and this underscored his need to be even more competitive to make his own way in the world.

"Not only was he not selected, he also despaired as his parents scrounged around helplessly for contacts they simply didn't have," writes Thomas F. O'Boyle in *At Any Cost*. "The two successful nominees went to prestigious private schools— one to Columbia and the other to Tufts—while Jack, who had had his heart set on Dartmouth, enrolled at the state University of Massachusetts at Amherst."[5] This incident—along with other experiences such as working as a $3-a-day caddy for wealthy golfers at the local country club—reinforced Welch's self-image as one "who always had [his] nose pressed up against the glass."

Yet Welch always tried to turn weakness or disappointment into advantage. His summers as a golf caddy helped him find and learn a sport at which he could become considerably better than average. And he later realized that attending U. Mass. instead of Dartmouth or MIT put him in a much better position to rise to the top than he would have had at more competitive campuses. *Play in games you can win* was a lesson in life that Welch applied with great results in business.

When Welch enrolled at the University of Massachusetts in the fall of 1953, he became the first member of his family ever to attend college. He did very well there, landing on the dean's list, earning a B.S. in chemical engineering with honors and scholarships to graduate school.

Welch chose the University of Illinois, arriving there in 1957 and leaving three years later with a Ph.D. in chemical engineering, a wife (Carolyn, whom he married in 1959), and a new Volkswagen Beetle his proud father gave him as a graduation present. Emerging from his education in 1960 with an advanced degree in a sought-after field, "Dr." Welch received three job offers. Fatefully—for him, for the company, and for the global business community of the late 20th century—he chose General Electric.

TAKE THIS RAISE AND SHOVE IT!

JACK WELCH REPORTED for work at General Electric's Plastics Division in Pittsfield, Massachusetts, drawing an annual salary of $10,500. There was no indication that this was the start of a 41-year career, all at the same company, with 20 of those years spent in the corner office. Welch remembers his initial career goal in simple terms: "I wanted to make $30,000 by the time I was 30."[6]

His assignment was a good one. Plastics were just emerging as the most important and prevalent material in manufacturing.

At GE's Plastics Division, Welch was asked to develop new materials and markets for these products. Within a year, it became clear to his superiors that Welch not only had solid technical abilities but good instincts for markets, sales, and management as well. A steady but slow climb up GE's formidably long management ladder was in the cards.

But Welch was in a hurry. He knew he was good. He was confident in his contributions—and he wanted to be rewarded and promoted accordingly. So when he was given only a $1,000 raise after his first year for what he thought was a standout performance, he was angry and wanted to know why. The answer made him even angrier—so angry that he turned in his resignation and accepted a chemical engineering position at International Mining and Chemicals in Chicago.

What made him so furious? Being told that the customary practice at GE was to give everyone the same raise, in the interests of fairness and harmony. Welch was disgusted by the idea that regardless of performance and ability the rewards were the same for all.

GE didn't want to lose Welch, and at a private dinner with his vice president and the two men's wives just before his departure, they came to terms. Welch would get a bigger raise and a better title and would stay at General Electric.

The incident played a seminal role in Welch's own management and compensation practices as chairman of GE years later, when he devised and championed a corporate meritocracy. At Welch's GE, the brightest lights were promoted fast and compensated spectacularly. The worst were fired.

Welch's attempted resignation from General Electric also reveals one of the most telling indicators and requisites for today's leaders—sometimes you have to be willing to put it all on the line for what you believe. That doesn't mean threatening to quit or digging in your heels over every small disagreement. But on the big issues where fundamental principles are involved, a key test in both leadership and personal conduct is the willingness to walk away from intolerable or unacceptable behavior even when the price is high. Doing that could very well work out and pay off, as it did for young Jack Welch in 1961. But there are no guarantees.

A RAPID RISE

ONCE HE AND GE kissed and made up, Welch rose quickly through the ranks in the Plastics Division and then in the company as a whole:

In 1963 he was placed in charge of chemical development in his division.

In 1968, at the age of 33, Welch became the youngest general manager ever, responsible for the whole Plastics Division.

In 1972 he became a company vice president.

In 1973 Welch was promoted to group executive, with management responsibilities for more than $1.5 billion in GE business.

In 1977 Welch became senior vice president for consumer products and services and also vice chairman of the GE Credit Corporation.

In 1979 he was appointed vice chairman and executive officer for General Electric.

In 1981, at age 45, he became the eighth and youngest chairman of General Electric.

Welch knows he owes much of his rapid rise at GE to the creative, freewheeling, and often contentious culture he found and helped magnify at the Plastics Division. To this day he describes Plastics as his "favorite business" at GE. When corporate headquarters relocated to Fairfield, Connecticut, in the mid-1970s, Welch stayed in Pittsfield—where he figured he could enjoy more autonomy. That finally changed in 1977 when GE Chairman Reginald Jones told Welch flat out that if he wanted to be in the running for the top job, he'd better relocate himself and his family to Fairfield.

The Welches were soon on their way to Fairfield.

THE OUTSIDER MOVES IN

AS NOTED IN chapter 14, Welch learned a lot about how to handle his own selection of a successor by the way his predecessor, Reg Jones, handled his. It was a careful and deliberate process that began just two years after Jones took over. It was also a consciously triggered competition among six top GE executives, stage-managed and refereed by Jones. This had to be good news for the relentlessly competitive Jack Welch.

Yet Welch was considered the underdog. "Welch was the definite dark horse and had little enthusiastic support at the very top of the corporation," explains O'Boyle.[7] Part of the cool reception was due to class and cultural factors, he believes. "As a group, CEOs tend to come from the upper strata of society; studies have shown the rich and upper-middle class to be over-represented among American CEOs by a considerable margin."[8]

But bigger questions surrounded Welch's style and personality. Would they mix with the staid and decorous GE culture? No one doubted that Welch had delivered solid results in all his assignments—but a good deal of his reputation, both positive and negative depending on who's doing the evaluating, sprang from his dynamic personality.

O'Boyle, a Welch critic, articulates the personality factor this way: "One of his charms was that he didn't try to sublimate his personality or his passion; what you saw was what you got. What you saw was a man whose forceful personality made him appear somewhat bigger than he was."[9]

In a world full of cloying insincerity, particularly in business and politics, many of us read characterizations like that and say, "Amen!" Indeed, the energy, the drive, the ambition, coupled with the ability to look reality square in the eye and tell it like it is helped endear Welch to legions of fans inside and outside GE throughout his tenure as chairman. The Welch persona contains many facets that suggest the kind of qualities that comprise today's successful leader.

It was never his looks nor the physical impression he makes when entering a room. "If you passed him on the street you would see little to identify him . . . as a corporate chairman—unless you caught the intense look in his piercing blue-green eyes," a *Washington Post* reporter wrote back in 1984.[10]

He is blunt and brash but his people could always argue back. Despite his toughness and the sometimes brutal judgments he made about others' performance and abilities, he invested enormously in coaching and training and engaged in many acts of personal kindness. On one occasion during a plant visit in St. Louis, a manager confessed to Welch how nervous he was in advance of Welch's trip and how his nonstop work on a presentation to the CEO had made life miserable at home for his wife. On the way back home in the company plane, Welch arranged for roses and a bottle of Dom Perignon to be delivered to the manager's wife along with a handwritten note of apology.[11]

He was always competitive, often relentlessly so—but with age and success he became more good-natured about it. An accomplished golfer, he's proud of his prowess on the course—as revealed in an incident that occurred when in 1996, *Golf Digest* magazine named Sun Microsystems chief Scott McNealy number one in a ranking of top CEO golfers. Welch ranked second. McNealy, knowing Welch's competitive nature and wanting some face time with the GE leader, challenged him to a round of golf. Welch eagerly accepted and beat McNealy. Later, he put McNealy on the GE board.[12]

He always seemed to be everywhere, performing many tasks at once, engaging people at levels of his organization and beyond in constant interaction. "I've never met anybody . . . who could simultaneously focus on so many different things," wrote journalist Holly Peterson in London's *Independent* in 2000. "For lunch it's always a turkey sandwich, lettuce and tomato on whole wheat, with mustard. He eats at his desk while he's on the phone. And he's a fast eater."[13] From daily workouts at the GE gym to golf and ski weekends, CEO Welch was always on the go.

Throughout his tenure, little slowed him down or seemed to distract him from GE for very long. When he had triple by-pass surgery in May 1985 he was fully up to speed by Labor Day. Also in 1985 Jack and Carolyn Welch divorced after 28 years of marriage and four children. A new romance bloomed, thanks to the matchmaking skills of former Citicorp Chairman Walter Wriston and his wife. In 1989, Welch married investment banker Jane Beasley, whom the Wristons had introduced to him.

And no detail seemed too small. *Today Show* host Matt Lauer tells the story about the time he played a foursome of golf with Welch. Another CEO in the group used the occasion to complain that his wife was having problems with her GE dishwasher. Lauer couldn't believe that such a subject had been raised with the head of the most valuable corporation in the world. He asked Welch what he was going to do and the GE leader replied, "I'm going to have her dishwasher fixed."[14]

Yet in the context of GE's CEO-selection process in the late 1970s, traits that now look like mostly positive qualities of Welch's distinct leadership style looked to many like negatives. Welch's problem, in O'Boyle's words, was that he was "the antithesis of everything GE represented at that time. . . . Speed was the very essence of the man. He rushed ahead, sometimes impetuously, and flouted convention."[15]

Welch's strong, bull-in-a-china-shop personality initially troubled Reg Jones as well and the CEO reportedly had strong reservations about tapping him. Welch's support on GE's board was minimal.

Jones later came around to back Welch, convinced that the rougher edges of Welch's personality would be a small price to pay for the tremendous energy and intelligence that went with them.

Subsequent interviews with the leading contenders convinced Jones that Welch also had that "vision thing"—a quality that would be so critical for a business leader in a ceaseless spiral of change. When Jones posed the hypothetical question—"Who should run GE if you and I are flying together in the company plane and it crashes?—Welch refrained from evaluating the other candidates and focused on the big picture trends that would buffet the company and the changes GE would have to make to prosper in a new environment.

It still took another year for Jones to sell his choice to the board of directors. On April 1, 1981, Jack Welch—the dark horse, the outsider, the son of a train conductor, the yearning soul who always had his "nose pressed against the glass"— walked into the chairman's office for the first time as GE's new leader. Few people beyond Jones and the inner circle knew he was about to start a revolution there.

CHAPTER 4

MESSING WITH SUCCESS

The very essence of leadership is that you have to have a vision.
You can't blow an uncertain trumpet.
—FATHER THEODORE M. HESBURGH

W HEN 45-YEAR-OLD Jack Welch walked into the office on April 1, 1981, to assume his new post as chairman of General Electric, the venerable corporation was in pretty good shape. It was a profitable and successful company, respected for its history and its steady if unspectacular performance through the years. Investors could point to 26 straight quarters of improved earnings, and they'd enjoyed uninterrupted quarterly dividends for decades—increases during every quarter since 1975.

GE's leadership was respected as well. In 1982, looking back on former CEO Reginald Jones's era as it tried to get a handle on Welch, the *Wall Street Journal* wrote that Jones "left a legacy of management skill so respected that other corporations paid GE to teach them its techniques—or better yet, wooed away a GE executive."[1]

From Reginald Jones to the more than 400,000 employees toiling in its factories, labs, and offices around the world, GE people were generally known for their dedication, professionalism, and concern with quality and customer. And GE was an American company through and through, with more than 80 percent of its revenues generated domestically, mostly in the fundamental industries that had turned an agrarian America into the world's industrial giant during the first half of the 20th century.

GE on April 1, 1981, was safe, solid, staid, respectable—perhaps a little boring but always dependable.

And Jack Welch saw it as a company clinging to a dying past. "We've long believed that when the rate of change inside an institution becomes slower than the rate of change outside, the end is in sight. The only question is when," he wrote to share owners in February 2001. By that yardstick, the safe and solid company Welch inherited in 1981 was in big trouble.

During the years just prior to his ascension, the U.S. economy had been slammed by double-digit inflation, 21-percent interest rates, and high unemployment. Diplomatic personnel were held hostage in Iran and the Soviets invaded Afghanistan, prompting the United States to boycott the 1980 Olympics.

Meanwhile the Japanese and Germans had moved their export-driven economies into high gear. The Japanese, in particular, were gobbling up the U.S. car market—capitalizing on American automakers' failure to respond quickly to the demand for fuel-efficient vehicles. Consumer electronics, finance, and real estate were set to follow in the 1980s. In promising third-country markets, Japanese and Europeans made major inroads, leaving most U.S. firms in the dust.

On the brighter side, the late 1970s also brought a wave of long-overdue deregulation of key industries such as aviation and trucking. With the election of Ronald Reagan in 1980, deregulation accelerated and spread throughout the economy.

But Welch knew that even this positive process would be painful. Less competitive companies would be gone. And the process of wringing the double-digit inflation out of the economy, engineered by Federal Reserve Board Chairman Paul Volcker, was sure to be painful as well. (It was. By 1982 the economy was in recession with over 10 percent of Americans unemployed.) During his interview with Jones during the successor selection process, Welch had said straight out that the company was too slow and too bureaucratic to prosper in this new environment.

And to top it all off just two days before Welch's new job began, President Reagan—less than 100 days into his term—was shot in the chest while leaving a Washington, D.C., hotel.

Such was the world Jack Welch saw around him as he plotted General Electric's future. The business environment for the rest of the century grew no calmer; it was marked by tumultuous change—good and bad change. A new, free-wheeling environment where the old rulebooks were thrown away was unfolding, brought about first by Reaganism and later by the onslaught of new technology. GE had to change with it—not out of fear but out of necessity. Not only to survive, but to prosper.

And so Jack Welch set out to mess with success. He made GE change before it really had to. He convinced GE watchers inside and outside the company to see problems where they saw none, to join him in a revolution when in fact most were quite satisfied with their current situation.

His ultimate goal was to create a company culture that not only accepted change but loved it. He knew it would be a tough task. "Learning to love change is an unnatural act in any century-old institution," he acknowledged as he looked back from the vantage point of 2001. "But today we have a Company that does just that: sees change always as a source of excitement, always as opportunity, rather than as threat or crisis."[2]

NEUTRON JACK, TRADER JACK

JACK WELCH AND GE traveled a long road to reach the point of "loving change." In the early days of his tenure, with complacency inside his organization and churning change outside, Welch all but blew up GE—shedding workers, eliminating layers of management, getting rid of underperforming businesses and buying new ones that didn't seem to fit the GE mold.

He paid a high price in the early years in image and reputation, becoming a poster boy for the ruthless corporate cost-cutting that many Americans associate with what came to be called the "Decade of Greed"—the 1980s. Welch did not invent concepts like downsizing and restructuring, but he was among the executives most associated with those controversial ideas. Many believed they were painful but necessary exercises to wring the fat and inefficiency out of the U.S. economy and save American industry in a new era of global competition. Others saw them as devious devices to boost profits and the bank accounts of the Wall Street crowd at the expense of average employees. More dispassionate critics wondered whether corporate America was paying too high a price in terms of lost employee loyalty and lost humanity.

Jack Welch stood at the center of the firestorm of controversy and debate. One magazine named him the "toughest boss in America." In CEO circles there could be some bragging rights in such a label. Even some Wall Street analysts—today among Welch's most enthusiastic supporters—wondered, "Why are you doing this, Jack?" Leave a good thing alone, they seemed to suggest.

As chronicled by Thomas F. O'Boyle in *At Any Cost,* Welch's first big attempt to make his case to the analysts that General Electric was in fact in trouble and that drastic change was necessary came in December 1981, in a speech in New York City. "The analysts, though, didn't get it," O'Boyle reports. "The speech was deemed a flop, and Welch was crushed."[3] Still he moved swiftly to implement the plans and strategies unveiled in that speech. GE businesses that weren't number one or number two in their markets—and had no chance of becoming so—would be fixed, sold, or closed. Excess rank-and-file and management employees would be let go. By the end of 1982, GE's workforce had been reduced by 35,000. Another 37,000 were cut the following year. By 1987, after more than five years as chairman, Welch had cut one out of every four GE workers, reducing the workforce by 100,000. The corporate staff was slashed from over 1,700 to 1,000.

During that same period revenues grew 48 percent, winning over most Wall Street analysts—who now suddenly did "get it." But to other observers, revenue growth in the face of major workforce reductions was no badge of honor. Instead they wondered why it was necessary to disrupt so many lives.

A 1987 blast by a union leader was typical of the heat Welch's moves generated. "The General Electric Company has a disease—Welch-it-is—caused by corporate greed, arrogance and contempt for its employees," he told *Business Week*.[4] But what cut most deeply was the moniker anonymously coined by a disgruntled GE employee—Neutron Jack. The name suggested that Welch's goal at the company was similar to that of the neutron bomb—destroy the people inside the buildings and plants, but leave the physical structures intact.

Welch loathed the label but it stuck. "It's a catchy tag. But it misses the point," he told a reporter in 1984. "It's a very unappealing name. It isn't the way it is."[5] Observed friend Walter Wriston, former chairman of Citicorp: "Whoever hung the name Neutron Jack on was a clever wordsmith, but it didn't have much to do with what was going on. Jack listens to the guy on the shop floor, to the fellow he meets, to everybody."[6]

He had less concern for those who said he was destroying an American icon by selling old GE businesses such as housewares and television. *Trader Jack,* that group called him. The products he was selling off were intertwined with the company's good name, its legacy, and its history. When he sold GE's consumer electronics business, some accused him of surrendering to the Japanese. "It's disturbing that a company of GE's demonstrated historical competence apparently shies away from competing in manufacturing," another executive anonymously complained to the *Los Angeles Times*.[7]

Welch appeared unfazed by such analysis or sentimentality. In his first two years alone, he sold 71 businesses and entered 118 new ones through acquisitions, partnerships, and joint ventures. Downsize, consolidate, simplify—pick winners and discard losers: In this fashion, Welch believed, he would build a more globally competitive company that would generate enough cash to attract investors, provide the resources to seize new opportunities quickly, and attract the best employees from all over the world. He wasn't nuking workers, he was saving the company. Companies can't guarantee employment, only customers can, he liked to say.

Some observers grasped Welch's vision early on, but it took time to enable most to understand that the overall renovation of American business led by Welch and others was necessary for the United States to restore its productivity and regain its competitiveness. The historic prosperity of the 1990s is testament to the fact the investment paid off.

"Farsighted, incisive—and controversial—he recognized the threat of competition from Japan and elsewhere and had the intellectual and emotional strength to deal with it," opined a writer in *Time* magazine in 1998. "He set the tone for U.S. industry. GE became highly productive by undertaking a complex reorganization that simplified the company into one with dominant positions in its carefully chosen businesses."[8]

Interestingly, one individual who endorsed Welch's moves early on and understood his reasons for them was his predecessor, Reginald Jones. This support was important to Welch and he returned the favor by offering nothing but praise for Jones's own service to the company.

"I became very concerned that the technologies in which GE was most involved were changing and changing fast," Jones told the *Washington Post* in 1984. "We were looking at slower growth, intensified competition—particularly international—

and a much higher technological content."[9] To Jones that meant the company needed someone at the top who could keep up with the change. That meant Jack Welch. "Jones was realistic enough to know that the company needed something more" than the "military-style command-and-control systems" he had put in place, a *Fortune* magazine analysis reasoned in 1989. "In choosing Welch as his successor, he went for an engineer who was comfortable with technology, had a record of sizzling financial performance, and was a proven master at managing change."[10]

Even though there were sharp contrasts in the two men's temperaments and style, Jones quite uncannily understood that Welch's hard-charging, irreverent personality would be right for the times. "I also saw in Jack a tremendous amount of drive, and against this era of slower growth . . . we were looking for speed. And that drive was going to help us achieve that speed," Jones explained.[11]

As for the charge that Welch was forsaking GE's legacy by shunning traditional businesses in favor of less orthodox ones, Jones insisted that his successor, who spent his entire career at the company, was very much imbued with the GE culture. "He's infected with the culture that exists," Jones said. "This culture gives us some common bonds; it holds us together."[12]

WITHSTANDING THE HEAT

BY FORCING SUCH fundamental change on an institution that didn't see the need for much change and by triggering a firestorm of criticism as he pushed the changes through,

Welch's mettle as a leader was tested early on. His actions and reactions suggest some of leadership's most important premises in today's environment:

Leaders change before they have to. They look over the horizon and prepare today to meet tomorrow's challenges.

Leaders don't back down in the face of criticism. They stay the course.

Leaders love change. They embrace it. They turn it into opportunity.

But leaders are not so arrogant to think they can control change or even always predict it. "We're no better prophets than anyone else, and we have difficulty predicting the exact course of change," Welch told his shareholders in 2001. "But we don't have to predict it. What we have to do is simply jump all over it!"[13]

Indeed Welch seems to have little use for endless long-range planning documents produced by company planners or prognostications spun by futurists. "Predictions of trends and megatrends are in full production," he noted in his letter to share owners for 1998. "Their record for accuracy has been spotty at best."[14] Upon becoming chairman of GE in 1981 one of Welch's quickest and most drastic actions was to decimate the ranks of the corporate planning department built up by Jones.

Leaders make the change and later . . . they change the change! From his earliest days in the corner office, Welch plotted and led a company revolution. He withstood enormous pressure and harsh criticism to make GE more competitive. He rid it of losing businesses and excess cost. He entered new ventures that put it on the path to becoming a truly global company with a mix of services, technology, and manufacturing businesses that fit a new competitive environment. It was a painful revolution but it kept paying off in the form of a more profitable and competitive company.

So what did Jack Welch do as soon as the fruits of his revolution began to flower? He started a new revolution!

THE SECOND REVOLUTION

DOWNSIZING AND restructuring were never ends in themselves. Any fool with a thick skin can cut cost out of an organization. But you can't cut your way to profitability, growth, or success. That required a different kind of change at GE. By the late 1980s, Welch had essentially completed his structural revolution at GE and initiated a cultural revolution.

It revolved around people. "The decade of the 1980s imposed two distinct challenges," Welch explained. "In the first phase, through 1986, we had to pay attention to the hardware—fixing businesses.

"In the second phase, from 1987 well into the 1990s, we've had to focus on the software. Our sustained competitiveness can only come from improved productivity, and that requires the bottom up initiatives of all our people."[15]

Welch's focus on "software" would spawn initiatives like Work-Out, Six Sigma, the Crotonville training sessions, and the creation of a meritocracy at GE that emphasized not only bottom-line results but values as well. These "software" programs will be examined more closely in Chapters 8 through 10. As the world went crazy over Internet technology in the 1990s, with the IT manager being seen as the most important person in many companies, Welch instead focused on human behavior and by his own admission was a late arrival to the Internet revolution.

Observers quickly noticed the new emphasis on the "softer" values of empowering people at all levels of GE, rewarding ideas and placing a premium on mentoring and coaching. Had Jack Welch changed, they wondered? Had he gone soft? Was he deliberately trying to reengineer his own image?

"Nah," says Welch. "I haven't changed a thing!" He adds, "I try to adapt to the environment I'm in. In the 70s, when I was helping grow new businesses—at plastics, medical—I was a wild-eyed growth boy. And then I got into the bureaucracy and I had to clean it out, so I was different in 1981. And now I'm in another environment. But that's not being 'born again.'"[16]

Still the metamorphosis of the Welch image from that of corporate axeman in the early 1980s to the empowering people person of the late 1990s is remarkable. Whereas other cost-cutters of that earlier decade were never able to move past their initial reputations ("Chainsaw" Al Dunlop, for example), Welch had the agility to evolve with the changing times. It helps explain his virtually unprecedented longevity as a corporate CEO.

After all, if the environment can change once, it can change again. Recent history is replete with examples of companies, organizations, governments, political administrations, and even figures in sports and entertainment who were pioneers in their fields, but then become "extinct volcanoes." They pushed the need to change on themselves, their teams, their audiences, and those they led—and then forgot their own lessons and grew complacent and arrogant. In some cases they lost their energy, their nerve, and their keen sensitivity to the world around them.

Welch was determined not to let this happen to himself or General Electric. He was determined to be a change agent until the very end, always restless and always searching for the next hot concept, the next big idea.

Through his willingness to mess with GE's success and change a company most were satisfied with, by making tough decisions and taking the heat, and then doing it all over again with relish, Welch demonstrated critical qualities for success and leadership. If you don't love change it won't love you—and it might just eat you alive!

WELCH ON LEADERSHIP: CHANGE BEFORE YOU HAVE TO

- Don't be satisfied with the status quo, even when it looks pretty good.

- Try to anticipate the environment in which you and your organization will operate in the near-term future and prepare for it.

- Don't be discouraged if you can't accurately forecast change—even the experts often miss the boat—but be flexible and adaptable to the change that comes.

- Be prepared to make tough decisions. Don't back down just because you are criticized or attacked. The most popular leaders are not necessarily the best leaders.

- Compete with a vengeance—but pick battles you have a shot at winning.

- Don't become complacent after leading your organization to significant and successful change. You will soon have to do it again!

CHAPTER 5

MAN OF IDEAS, MAN OF ACTION

Be willing to make decisions. That's the most important quality in a good leader. Don't fall victim to what I call the "ready-aim-aim-aim syndrome." You must be willing to fire.
—T. BOONE PICKENS

JACK WELCH WAS A serial revolutionary at GE, a perpetual change agent. Summing up his era at the company, *Business Week* reported: "A brash upstart who was inimical to the staid GE culture, he started his tenure at the top by ruthlessly cutting corporate fat during the 1980s, earning unparalleled infamy among the rank and file.

"But that downsizing positioned GE for the '90s boom. And now that he has added almost $500 billion in shareholder value, the slasher image has long since been replaced by that of a management savant."[1]

And a key component of the leadership formula that transformed Welch into a management guru and attracted legions of followers is the role that ideas play in his leadership style—

big, bold, brash ideas. Sometimes brilliant ideas, sometimes bad ideas, but just as important, the courage to act on them.

As he rose through the ranks at GE, Welch looked like a wild man to many of his colleagues—and in an important sense he lived up to that image. His conception of leadership is entirely different from those who believe the person at the top must deliberate, dispassionately choose an organization's course, and rein in more rambunctious underlings. At Welch's GE, if anyone were to need reining in it would be the chairman himself.

"One of the things about leadership is that you cannot be a moderate, balanced, thoughtful, careful articulator of policy," he explains. You've got to be on the lunatic fringe."[2]

General Electric is a manufacturing company, a services company, and a media company—but Welch saw its most important identity as an idea company. He poured time and resources into building what he hoped would be the most productive idea factory in the world—with himself serving as shop steward. Ideas were the currency of success at GE and Welch personally meant to ensure that the company generated piles of that currency.

"My job is to find great ideas, exaggerate them, and spread them like hell around the business at the speed of light," he once enthused. In his value system, "The hero is the one with the best ideas."[3] He rewarded people accordingly, even when the ideas did not pan out.

"We look everywhere for a better idea. We come to work knowing there's a better way every day," he told the *Australian Financial Review* in 2000.[4] "We believe it. We search the world for the best idea."

Yet don't for a moment think that Welch had any interest in running an ivy tower think tank. Standing at the plate is not enough; you have to be willing to swing the bat. Hit a home run or strike out—don't just stand there and refuse to swing. "Jack grew up in an environment that encouraged people to take chances," remarked a GE senior vice president back in 1984. "That's almost religious with him now. He almost goes overboard. You find a guy who took a big swing and didn't make it, he gets management awards."[5] Another colleague explained: "One of the fundamental things about Welch is that he doesn't have a fear of being wrong."[6]

Welch has quibbled with the characterization that he is a risk taker and has actually criticized himself for moving too slowly on occasion! But he confirms his sentiment for the big strike-out. "I've rewarded failures by giving out awards to people when they failed because they took a swing. Keep taking swings."[7]

The image of the leader as an individual of bold moves and big strokes, an action-oriented individual who would rather play than sit on the sidelines, holds special appeal in today's culture. Whether on television, in politics, or in government and office bureaucracies, we see a world full of talkers and few doers. We see many rear-end coverers and few risk takers. We see legions of bootlickers and a thin scattering of independent thinkers. We hear a lot of reasons why things can't be done and precious few suggestions about what *can* be done.

Jack Welch provides a model of a leader who believes in action, not just talk. He was always positive, enthusiastic—on the edge and sometimes over the top. For those who, either because of circumstance or personality, have been consigned to somewhat lower altitudes, it can be refreshing, exciting, and even inspiring to watch a self-described lunatic in action—

particularly when his theater is the normally dull and pre-dictable world of big business.

And a leader must make decisions and make them with dispatch. Welch showed a clear dislike for the manager who says maybe. It's a word that barely exists in his vocabulary. "Welch will say yes. Welch will say no. But he never says maybe," an executive told *Business Week* in 1998. Another wryly remarked: "Jack is not famous for patience . . . which is an understatement." In one example cited by the magazine, executives at GE Capital had spent months examining the prospects of buying AT&T's Universal Credit Card and de-cided they wanted to go ahead. They made a detailed presen-tation to Welch who gave them an answer within 24 hours—no.[8]

A WELCH GRAND SLAM

THE BUSINESS WORLD didn't have to wait too long for Welch to demonstrate what he meant by living on the "lunatic fringe." His drastic early moves to trim and slim GE so it could compete in the global marketplace shocked the culture of a company that was accustomed to far more incremental moves. "Skip the incremental and go for the leap," was his credo.[9]

That's exactly what Welch did in December 1985 when he called a press conference in New York City to announce that General Electric would purchase RCA and its crown jewel, NBC, for $6.28 billion. The purchase was made possible by the savings the company realized from its downsizing efforts over the preceding four years.

At the time it was the biggest non-oil merger ever. GE was now in the media and entertainment business and also owned in RCA the top-selling television brand.[10]

The move knocked the socks off Wall Street and established Welch's reputation early on as a master of the big deal. Meshing his style and the GE culture with that of NBC was another matter. Purists in the newsroom in particular resented the cost controls and budget cuts that Welch imposed, but as both GE and NBC grew more successful, the marriage proved fulfilling for all.

Even Welch critic Thomas F. O'Boyle acknowledged, "The turnaround at NBC illustrated the positive aspects of Welch's management style: his ability to inspire and win the enthusiasm of people; his willingness to take chances in support of their efforts; and his penchant, zeal even, or fast-paced, action-based decision-making."[11]

Yet Welch being Welch, he could never really leave a great thing alone. He once even tried his hand at creative programming, suggesting to NBC entertainment executives that they create a television series based on the Michael Douglas movie, *Wall Street*. When they lambasted—even ridiculed—the idea a good-natured but humbled Welch said, "I'm going back to businesses where people listen to me."[12]

Despite NBC's climb back to the top of the ratings heap, in the 1990s consolidation of media businesses into multimedia communications giants was the trend and Jack Welch took a stab at joining it when he met with Disney's Michael Eisner in 1994. As Welch attempted to sell Disney a share of NBC with many conditions attached, Eisner experienced firsthand the infectious quality of Welch's enthusiasm and love of the big deal done fast.

"Jack had me wrapped around his little finger. I was all excited about this," he recalls. "He completely convinced me it was a great deal. I was ready to go."

But the magic started wearing off as soon as Eisner got in the elevator. He realized that Welch had sold him on a one-sided deal. When he called the GE executive the next day to decline, Welch just laughed in a way that seemed to convey "Oops, you caught me!"[13]

The outcome for the remainder of the RCA purchase was different. In what is seen as another example of Welch's fondness for the lunatic fringe, he sold the consumer electronic business, including the RCA television business with its number one 17-percent domestic market share, to the French-owned Thomson S.A. The key component of the deal was that GE would acquire in exchange its X-ray and diagnostic equipment company, CGR. The acquisition proved to be fraught with problems and a financial drain. Welch "traded a sound business for an unsound business," opined O'Boyle, a view shared by others.[14]

STRIKING OUT

WELCH'S RAPID-FIRE decision making led to dozens if not hundreds of good business deals during his tenure. But as the consumer electronics/CGR trade reveals, there is a downside risk to Welch's approach. When you shun the incremental in favor of the quantum leap, the odds are strong that in a significant share of your leaps, you're going to fall flat on your face.

General Electric's purchase of the Kidder Peabody brokerage firm in 1986—and the scandal there in 1994 that cost GE over a billion dollars, destroyed Kidder, and damaged Welch's business reputation—is one such example. As I'll discuss further in Chapter 7, it also raised questions about another core tenet of Welch's leadership philosophy—his rejection of and revulsion for bureaucracy.

To Welch, one of the advantages of GE's size is its ability to withstand the occasional strikeout. "The biggest advantage of size is to go to bat more often," he said. "Because the more often you swing, the more often the chances are you'll get some hits."[15]

He even sees leadership value in having his troops see him fall flat from time to time. Referring to the Kidder purchase and ensuing scandal, he remarked: "I can talk to employees all the time and say if your chief executive can make the biggest mistake your company has ever made, you shouldn't be too frightened to take a swing."[16]

GOING OUT WITH A BANG

ANOTHER EPISODE was the move that Jack Welch hoped to wave goodbye with—his breathtaking $45 billion bid to acquire Honeywell.

The manner in which the deal unfolded was vintage Welch—a dramatic display of the swashbuckling CEO in action. In the fall of 2000 he learned of Honeywell's impending deal with United Technologies, a longtime GE rival, just days before it was to be finalized. When details of UT's offer leaked, Welch spent a frantic weekend trying to put together a better offer of his own, calling his board members on his cell phone while rushing between social engagements. When he learned that Honeywell's executive committee was sealed off in a conference room making their final decision on UT's offer, he convinced an assistant to interrupt the meeting so he could inform them he had a better offer. He scrawled the numbers on a piece of paper and faxed them over.[17]

In a stunning turnaround, Honeywell accepted GE's offer after UT refrained from entering a bidding war with that "wild man" at GE who was loaded down with cash. "It was nice of Mr. Welch to validate our business judgment—and to overpay," UT's CEO George David pointedly remarked.[18]

Honeywell's acceptance of Welch's last-minute offer was reportedly heavily influenced by his willingness to alter years of careful succession planning and agree to extend his tenure as CEO from a planned retirement in April 2001 to the end of that year. Welch informed his wife at dinner in a New York City restaurant. "It was very emotional for her in the restaurant. We had a different plan."[19]

Bold moves until the end—that was how Jack Welch intended to complete his business career. In one big stroke, he orchestrated one of the largest industrial mergers ever, displayed his fierce competitiveness one more time by besting a longtime rival, and upset the timetable for an event for which GE, the financial community, and his wife had been preparing for years—his retirement.

"The easiest thing in the world to do would have been to have not done this deal, retire with a band and have this great send off. 'See you later, Jack, great record,'" he reflected after the announcement.[20] He knew all along what was at stake: "I could have gone home early and been a great hero. I'm the one that's putting my neck on the line."[21]

By the spring of 2001, Welch learned how prescient he'd been. Though the merger was approved by U.S. officials, in the new global environment the company also needed the approval of European regulators. But they were balking at the deal, claiming that combining GE and Honeywell would create anticompetitive behavior.

In mid-June, Welch found himself in Brussels personally negotiating with taciturn E.U. officials and getting nowhere. Even offers to divest billions of dollars in Honeywell business failed to sway the regulators. The price they demanded for approval was so high it would have defeated the whole purpose of the merger. In a move reminiscent of President Reagan's Reykjavik walkout (leaving the 1984 summit when the Soviets demanded abandonment of the strategic defense initiative as the price of a new treaty), Welch walked away. As badly as he wanted the deal and as much as he had riding on it, he walked away.

The critics pounced with some justification. After all, many observers had predicted trouble with European regulators all along. "Mr. Welch, known for sizing up businesses in a heartbeat, misread the situation early on," claimed the *New York Times* in an article headed "A Rare Miscalculation for Jack Welch." "He failed to anticipate Europeans' anticompetitiveness concerns, saying regulators would find 'the cleanest deal you've ever seen.'"[22] An executive who advised Honeywell put it more bluntly, telling *Business Week* anonymously, "Although we all deify Jack, this was a very bad move."[23]

Reflecting on the crumbling of his last big deal, Welch was by turns defiant, philosophical, and self-deprecating. Asked why he chose to attempt such a giant leap at the end of his career, he said: "I had to do it. I'd do the same thing again tomorrow. I wasn't thinking about retiring. I was thinking about running GE. I took a shot at it. I gave it everything I had. And it wasn't enough."[24]

And referring to his plans to advise other companies on business strategy after his retirement from GE, Welch wryly suggested: "I don't think, in my new consulting business, that a lot of people will be interested in my advice on how to deal with the E.U."[25]

CREATING A STRETCH CULTURE

FROM THE BEGINNING to the end of his tenure as GE's chairman, Welch led by example. But he wanted the whole organization to reach high, to churn out new ideas, and to drive for the impossible. Watching the CEO do this was helpful and inspirational but not enough to instill a similar approach throughout the ranks. So Welch attempted to institutionalize boldness through a process he called "stretch."

Stretch "means moving beyond being as good as you have to be—'making a budget'—to being as good as you possibly can be: setting 'impossible' goals and going after them," he explained to shareholders in his letter dated February 9, 1996.[26] Workers and managers would, of course, have to keep their feet firmly planted on the ground, making their numbers and reaching their targets. But after that, Welch wanted to know, what was their stretch plan? What were the really big, long-shot goals they planed to strive for—and not just survive but prosper. What could they do that would turn themselves and their teams into stars?

"A stretch atmosphere replaces a grim heads-down determination to be as good as you have to be, and asks, instead, how good can you be?" he outlined in 1995. "Stretch in the simplest form, says, 'nothing is impossible,' and the setting of stretch targets inspires people and captures their imagination."[27]

Recognizing that underlings have less maneuvering room than the ones at the top and may be fearful of publicly stating grandiose goals for fear of failing and suffering the consequences, Welch insisted, "Whether we hit our targets or not is not the issue. What does matter is that we've broken out of a 110-year pattern with stretch thinking, and we're on to new targets."[28]

Deciding, doing, acting, and executing—in the Welch value system, these beat out talking, planning, and contemplating. Acting in the Welch fashion takes courage, hard work, and indefatigable energy. It's more than just a formula for effective and uplifting leadership; it suggests a mode of personal behavior many of us would like to see more of in ourselves. Big plans and good ideas are a dime a dozen—having the courage and discipline to act on them, even when comfort, security, and reputation are at stake, is much rarer.

WELCH ON LEADERSHIP: MAKING BIG DECISIONS

- Welch made good decisions and he made some bad ones, but he wasn't afraid to act.

- Leadership requires more than simply coming up with big ideas. You must have the courage to act on them—even when it means risking failure.

- Most people appreciate leaders who make decisions and set clear directions. They would rather their boss tell them no (accompanied by a reason) than get no feedback at all.

- Jack Welch said yes and he said no. He rarely said maybe.

- Successful leaders and organizations have two kinds of plans—the safe and sound one they need to run their organization on a day-to-day basis, and a "stretch" plan that contains dramatic, even outlandish goals and ideas. The stretch plan will not often be achieved but it excites, inspires, and pushes the organization higher.

- Leaders should reward people for thinking in an unorthodox fashion and for taking chances, even if an idea turns out to be a failure.

CHAPTER 6

MAKING THE ELEPHANT DANCE

Management is efficiency in climbing the ladder of success; leadership
determines whether the ladder is leaning against the right wall.
—STEPHEN R. COVEY

EMBRACING CHANGE, choosing action and speed over
talk and deliberation, and making big leaps instead of incremental steps served Jack Welch well as he transformed General Electric into an "accelerating cash and earnings engine."
But Welch achieved success not simply by doing what everyone else did only better. He did it by standing up and challenging the conventional wisdom—over and over again. By
moving in the opposite direction from the crowd. By antici-
pating a changing environment before others realized it and
acting upon that knowledge.

Yet as much as we tend to see someone who stands up to
the crowd in heroic terms, there are times when the crowd is
actually right. Just as most clichés become clichés because

they have at least some connection to reality, wisdom becomes conventional because enough people have enough empirical evidence to validate it. Indeed most discredited conventional wisdom falls not because it was *never* true but because it is *no longer* true.

So how adept was Welch at listening to the crowd when it was right? In the world of business, where the crowd is your customer base and consumer tastes, habits, and fears often override facts but must be catered to anyway, knowing when and how to listen and conform can make a critical difference in company profitability. For example, many consumers believe that genetically enhanced foods are somehow impure and unsafe. There is little if any evidence to back that up. But it's still "conventional wisdom," and a company like McDonald's felt it had to announce that it would not use such products at its restaurants.

Can leaders who buck trends, who challenge assumptions and swim against the tide, also know how to be good listeners, be open to the views of others and recognize when the consensus judgment is the right judgment? Or do they risk becoming so enamored with their image as professional contrarians— the lonely, principled opponents of the establishment—that they lose touch with reality and lose their credibility and effectiveness? Jack Welch offers some insights into this leadership conundrum.

JACK WELCH'S JURASSIC PARK

TO MANY OBSERVERS, Welch's most astounding achievement rests simply in the way he made his huge, lumbering conglomerate so successful in a business era that prizes core competencies, spin-offs, focus, and market segmentation. The conglomerate is out of favor in the high-speed, high-tech environment, with plenty of examples of failure to back up this conventional wisdom. Meanwhile Jack Welch seemed to be the curator of his own private corporate Jurassic Park where a dinosaur by the name of General Electric could survive, prosper, and sometimes terrorize its competitors at will.

Welch always denied his business model was headed for extinction—or for that matter, unique. "Our model is not in itself difficult to construct, nor are we the first to put together a mix of industrial/service/media and financial services businesses," he explained to shareholders in 1997. "It is the consistent aggregate performance of these large #1 or #2 businesses over a diverse array of global markets that makes this model work."[1]

During the mid-1990s, as many companies were spinning off large chunks of their business into separate entities or to other companies, Welch felt compelled to explain why GE was moving in the opposite direction. The subject was a major topic of his stockholders letter for 1995.

"The hottest trend in business in 1995," he acknowledged, "and the one that hit closest to home—was the rush toward breaking up multi-business companies and 'spinning-off' their components, under the theory that their size and diversity inhibited their competitiveness."

Welch knew that anxious investors would want to know if their company would be next.

"The short answer is that we're not. We've spent more than a decade getting bigger and faster and more competitive, and we intend to continue.

"Breaking up is the right answer for some big companies. For us it is the wrong answer."[2]

Welch was convinced he could continue to "make the elephant dance" as long as General Electric behaved like a small company even as it grew bigger. "What we are trying relentlessly to do is get that small-company soul and small-company speed inside our big-company body," he explained.[3] If he could foster an entrepreneurial culture—with all the inventiveness, risk taking, and fast-paced action such a culture brings—but still have the resources of a big company at his disposal, the combination would be dynamic and unbeatable. And General Electric's move past IBM in 1991 as the nation's most valuable company provided dramatic testimony that he might be right.

Besides, his push for future growth was not aimless. There was a rhyme and reason. For most of his tenure, his famous number one–number two rule was in force. A business would be fixed, sold, or closed unless it ranked first or second in the market or had a reasonable chance of getting there. Welch saw the transformation of the U.S. economy from manufacturing to services. Why allow yourself to become yesterday's news? GE should be a services company that also makes great products; that's how he liked to put it.

Speaking of news, the economy was also becoming information-driven, with data, financial transactions, and market intelligence moving like lightning around the globe in multimedia formats. GE must be a part of that movement too; hence the importance of NBC, its CNBC cable operation, and strategic partnerships with Microsoft and Dow Jones.

And he was excited by the growing market opportunities overseas. More than just missed export opportunities were at stake. He also understood that if the company didn't become a major global player, others who did would soon come hunting for GE's domestic markets. A big company had far greater resources and reach to capitalize on global opportunities in a big way.

Still, observers remain transfixed with how far out of style the Welch approach seems to be—and they wonder whether GE will retire the model along with him. "Being a conglomerate is now deeply unfashionable, but Welch has never been one to bow to market whims," wrote the *Times* of London in 2001.[4] *Business Week* makes a similar point and raises questions about the future: "The company is a glaring exception to Wall Street's preference for pure plays. . . . Holding that mass together may prove a challenge too daunting for anyone besides Welch." The magazine goes on to quote management expert James J. O'Toole, who had invoked an interesting analogy. "What this feels like is Yugoslavia when Tito died."[5]

During the December 2000 press conference where Welch introduced Jeffrey Immelt as his successor, Immelt was immediately peppered with speculative questions about the future of various GE businesses, from NBC to GE Capital. He understandably refused to engage in speculation at that early juncture. But many GE watchers, including *Business Week,* openly speculated whether Immelt would soon feel compelled to veer from Welch's path. "Given today's preference for highly focused companies, Immelt could face enormous pressure to sell chunks of GE," the magazine reported. "Especially if it fails to continue to meet investor expectations and maintain the gravity-defying stock multiples it enjoyed under Welch."[6]

As for Welch, as he confronted the growing fashion of corporate spin-offs in the mid-1990s, he made it clear there was only one kind of spin-off that really interested him:

"We are a Company intent on getting bigger, not smaller—a Company whose only answer to the trendy question, 'What do you intend to spin off?' is 'cash—and lots of it.'"[7]

JOINING THE CONSENSUS—
NUCLEAR POWER AND DEFENSE

IT'S NOT THAT Welch did nothing but add companies to General Electric's portfolio. He sold plenty of them, too—350 over the course of his tenure as chairman. Some, like the sale of GE Housewares to Black & Decker in 1984, deeply upset longtime guardians of the company flame who believed Welch had forsaken a proud part of GE's legacy. The business flopped at Black & Decker, which may indicate that, understandable sentimentality aside, Welch had accurately foreseen the division's narrow future.

Other sales showed a deft ability to jump onto an emerging conventional wisdom just as the train was leaving the station. General Electric's nuclear power business is a good example. After the Three Mile Island accident in 1977, the tide of popular opinion turned against the industry, despite its overall good safety record and proven ability to produce relatively cheap power without contributing to global warming. Welch saw the handwriting on the wall and sent a message to GE's world-class stable of nuclear scientists and engineers that they didn't want to hear or accept.

"When I said, in 1981, that there was not going to be another nuclear plant built in the United States, they were upset, they were angry, they were writing letters," he recalled. "I feel for them. It's a tough deal. But the world decided nuclear power was not what it wanted."[8] GE left the business, though it continued to maintain and equip the facilities it had already built.

In 1993, General Electric left another business it had been in a long time—the defense business. GE sold its aerospace division to Martin Marietta for some $4 billion. The cold war was over and defense cutbacks were under way. This— along with all the headaches GE's role as defense contractor had brought in terms of investigations, indictments, and scandals—convinced Welch it was time to get out.

GETTING RUN OVER— KIDDER PEABODY AND HONEYWELL

IF WELCH OFTEN BUCKED conventional wisdom when it would pay off and joined it when it made sense, on other occasions he ignored the consensus to his peril. In the process he had occasion to demonstrate how he met a critical test for any leader—reacting constructively to mistakes and failures and learning from them.

Plenty of eyebrows were raised when Welch decided he wanted GE to own a brokerage house—especially since that business was notoriously unstable and poorly monitored in the freewheeling 1980s. The skeptics appeared to be onto something when GE found itself having to infuse Kidder with cash upon closing the deal in 1986. The phantom trading and profits scandal that unfolded in 1994 not only broke Welch's string of uninterrupted quarters of earnings growth, it eventually forced him to fire the close colleague he'd placed in charge of the business.

Inside GE's inner sanctum, the unfolding Kidder mess reportedly triggered more than one outburst of the legendary Welch temper. To the outside world, he displayed a feisty acceptance of the mistake, an aggressive defense of his company's overall soundness, and above all a desire to put failure in the bottom drawer and move on.

When the *Wall Street Journal,* for example, asked Welch to respond to the suggestion that the Kidder fiasco was a sign he was losing his touch, he snapped, "Who says that? Be sure and quote them by name." He went on to urge, "Let's not focus on one bad tree in the forest."[9] And as the last chapter showed, Welch was eventually able to hold up the Kidder episode as an example to his troops where the boss made a big mistake but still kept taking big swings at big decisions.

Other observers noted the dispatch with which Welch moved to put the unpleasant past behind his company and move on. "When a similar crisis struck Salomon Brothers, major investor Warren Buffett stepped in and ran the company until its reputation was restored," Canada's *National Post* noted. "Mr. Welch would have none of that. He washed his hands of the affair and dumped Kidder as quickly as he could."[10]

In his 1994 letter to stockholders, released on February 10, 1995, Welch pronounced this simple benediction on the whole affair: "Whether or not it was a good idea to buy Kidder in 1986 is academic—in the end, it simply didn't work out."[11]

Surely, Welch never imagined that he would have to grapple with failure again at the very end of his tenure as chairman, but as discussed, that's exactly what happened in his daring but ultimately abortive attempt to acquire Honeywell. In this case it must be said that the conventional wisdom—at least externally—amply warned Welch and GE of possible serious problems in getting the deal approved by European regulators. He clearly didn't heed these warnings, but did he even hear them?

Welch indicates he was convinced there were no serious overlaps in the two companies' businesses worthy of triggering insurmountable objections by the E.U. And he suggests it was strong lobbying of the decision makers by GE's competitors (who didn't want the deal to go through) that turned the tide.

Whether or not such lobbying made the decisive difference, Welch's reaction to this and other rebuffs did reveal a headstrong resistance to accepting failure or defeat. But redeeming this impulse is the fact that he moved quickly to clean up errors and move on. And as with the Honeywell merger, when it came to a choice between creating the image of a triumph (giving E.U. regulators everything they wanted to salvage the deal) or walking away in defeat for the good of the company and his personal integrity, Welch walked away.

In a broad sense, Welch has been quite expansive on the subject of mistakes. "We've made millions of mistakes, missteps. We've made about every mistake there is to be made, I think. See, the luxury of being a big company is that you can go to bat often." Even while acknowledging errors, Welch was always pressing his advantage, turning weakness into strength.

"I don't mind being wrong. The key is to win a lot more than you lose."[12]

WELCH ON LEADERSHIP:
THE CONVENTIONAL WISDOM

- Jack Welch was not afraid to buck the conventional wisdom— a key trait of the successful leader.

- But on more than one occasion he learned the hard way that the conventional wisdom is sometimes right. One of the leader's most difficult challenges is to discern when the crowd is right and when it is wrong.

- Welch believes the best organizations are those that are big in resources, capital, and market reach—but that also maintain the characteristics of small organizations in their ability to capitalize on change and make and implement decisions quickly. Big companies can still be successful in more than one line of business if they are unified by common values.

- No one likes to admit they're wrong, and that includes Jack Welch, but Welch has demonstrated the importance of cleaning up and moving beyond mistakes quickly. Face up to failure and move on— and don't let it make you risk averse!

CHAPTER 7

JACK WELCH'S
WAR ON BUREAUCRACY

---

*We cultivate the hatred of bureaucracy in our Company and
never for a moment hesitate to use that awful word "hate."
Bureaucrats must be ridiculed and removed.*
—JACK WELCH IN HIS LAST LETTER TO
SHARE OWNERS, FEBRUARY 9, 2001

To SAY THAT Jack Welch loathes bureaucracy is an understatement. Over the course of his two decades as General Electric's leader, he kept adjusting his program to fit changing times. He became passionately enthused about new ideas while letting older ideas fade into the background. He let the tone, image, and style of his leadership soften over time as well.

But one thing that never changed or softened was his views about bureaucracy. As the chapter epigraph reveals, when it came to his campaign against unnecessary staff, process, and formality, there was no such animal as a "kinder, gentler" Jack Welch.

Bureaucrats "multiply in organizational layers and behind functional walls," he explained in that same letter, "which means that every day must be a battle to demolish this structure and keep the organization open, ventilated and free." Though he claimed considerable success at annihilating bureaucracy at GE and crowed about the Internet as the "final nail in the coffin" of bureaucracy, Welch also acknowledged its ability to make a comeback. At GE "people need to be vigilant—even paranoid—because the allure of bureaucracy is part of human nature and hard to resist, and it can return in a blink of an eye."[1]

In essence, Welch's plan was to replace the middle manager with direct communication and speed. He wasn't long into his tenure as CEO before other companies and the media noticed what he was up to. Though it was related to the restructuring and downsizing moves that focused on removing cost from the bottom line, Welch's war on bureaucracy was always much more. It was also an effort to create a culture of creativity, speed, informality, teamwork, and learning that he saw as absolutely essential to the survival and prosperity of large organizations in today's environment.

The passion Welch brought to this fight stemmed from his conviction that big companies that fail to act like small companies will not survive. His vision from the start was to have in GE "the soul of a small company in the body of a big one." Why was this so important? "Most successful small companies possess three defining cultural traits: self-confidence, simplicity and speed." Welch explained to share owners on February 9, 1996. "We wanted them. We went after them."[2]

DELAYERING

THE ANTI-BUREAUCRACY CAMPAIGN also sprang from personal experience—the frustrations he felt and observed firsthand as he rose in GE's ranks.

Growing up professionally in GE Plastics imbued Welch with a bitter distaste for corporate ritual and make-work projects. Plastics was considered a freewheeling, somewhat unruly place. Welch reportedly grew frustrated as he watched corporate overseers try to rein in the creative confusion.

"He remembers corporate staff 'bothering my people' by 'meddling and nitpicking,' demanding reports, presentations, facts and figures that contributed nothing to making and selling better products," reported *Business Week*. "He recalls how the businesses wasted time and energy cozying up to staff, throwing them lavish parties in hopes they'd be nice at appropriations time."[3] Welch still recalls and cites the example of the time the Light Bulb Division spent $30,000 on a promotional film to convince the corporate headquarters to approve new equipment.

Commenting later on the situation generally and reacting with visceral anger, Welch told *Fortune* magazine, "This internal focus has wasted our time, wasted our energy, frustrated us, made us so mad some nights over some bureaucratic jackass boss that we'd punch a hole in the wall."[4]

So it should have come as little surprise that upon assuming control of GE corporate headquarters, Welch slashed the corporate staff from 1,700 to 1,000 in his first year. Enter Welch's strategy of "delayering" General Electric.

"We delayered. We removed 'Sectors,' 'Groups,' 'Strategic Business Units' and much of the extensive command structure and staff apparatus we used to run the Company," he explained to shareholders on February 9, 1996.[5]

The concept had immediate practical impact. GE businesses no longer had to grind out monthly financial reports that no one used. Quarterly reports would do just fine. Managers had more time to run their operations. "We cleared out stifling bureaucracy, along with the strategic planning apparatus, corporate staff empires, rituals, endless studies and briefings, and all the classic machinery that makes big-company operations smooth and predictable—but often glacially slow," Welch elaborates.[6]

Remarked one GE executive about Welch's delayering strategy: "You know if he sees on a document that some poor guy needed 20 signatures to get something done, Jack will go into orbit. Next week there'll be one signature."[7]

WELCH INVENTS A NEW WORD

YET WELCH'S CULTURAL REVOLUTION at GE was more than one-dimensional (downsizing) and even more than two-dimensional (delayering, which means reducing the number of vertical levels of authority from the highest point to the lowest.) It is also three-dimensional, thanks to his newly coined word and awkwardly stated phrase—but powerfully evocative idea—called *boundaryless behavior.*

Boundaryless behavior, Welch explains, seeks to erase artificial lines that not only rope off employees within a company but the company from customers, other companies, and society. It's "one of the small company characteristics we've al-

ways coveted," he says. "It means simply the breaking or ignoring of artificial walls like functions, rank, geography, race,
sex and any other barrier in the way of a headlong rush toward the best ideas."[8]

The strategy fosters teamwork, solidarity, and intensity
within an organization. "We tear all the walls down and put
teams from all functions in one room to bring new products to
life. One room, one coffeepot, one team, one shared mission."

Boundarylessness not only smothers bureaucracy but also
smugness and complacency. "The sweetest fruit . . . has been
the demise of 'Not Invented Here' and its utter disappearance
from our Company,"[9] Welch asserted. Indeed he stated flat
out that many of GE's best practices and management improvements were invented elsewhere.

Welch always regarded it as a badge of honor to say you
were open and receptive to taking someone else's willingly
shared idea and making it your own. He credited companies
like American Standard, Caterpillar, Toshiba, and Wal-Mart
for generating innovative techniques that now bolster General
Electric's bottom line. In the case of Wal-Mart, Welch reported that its weekly direct customer feedback technique
called Quick Market Intelligence (QMI) was used produc-
tively at GE Appliances and especially at GE Capital's Re-
tailer Financial Services "to drive the quality of customer
service in its credit card operations and help grow earnings
more than 25 percent in 1994"[10]

SPEED, SIMPLICITY, SELF-CONFIDENCE

BY REMOVING BOTH vertical and horizontal barriers in
an organization like GE, Welch believes—with considerable

evidence to back him up—a new environment is created where better ways to do things are continually invented and refined. And what is just as important, once they appear, is that they can be implemented with speed, simplicity, and self-confidence.

It proved to be a matter of success and survival in an era when the only constant is change. "Today's global environment, with its virtually real-time information exchanges, demands that an institution embrace speed. Faster, in almost every case, is better," Welch said in 1995.[11] Bureaucracy, hierarchy, and the turf battles so endemic to sprawling and stratified institutions stand in the way of speed and thus success.

Welch points to examples such as GE Medical Systems, where product development went "from a two-year cycle to less than one." At GE's Appliance Division, the time it took to fill orders was cut from 18 months to just over three weeks.

How to get the job done and how to do it better were what interested Welch at GE. Strip away the jargon. Get rid of the make-work complications. That takes leaders who have absorbed all the information and good ideas they can from any and all sources and who then act with self-confidence.

"Self-confident people don't need to wrap themselves in complexity, 'businessese' speech, and all the clutter that passes for sophistication in business," Welch stated. So assertive was he on this point that he even stewed over the kind of language and terminology used by GE managers and engineers. "We are going to decomplicate everything we do and make at GE," he pledged to shareholders in 1995.

"Our communications with each other will be increasingly straightforward; our presentations to each other and to our customers will be simpler. Their richness will come from the dialogue, not the complexity of the charts."[12]

BEATING THE BUREAUCRACY— EASIER SAID THAN DONE

ALL THIS IS music to most people's ears. Do away with paperwork and process. Strip away the pretensions and the archaic procedures. Invite everyone to participate. Make decisions quickly and turn the institution around on a dime. After all, opposing bureaucracy is like opposing waste, fraud, and abuse in government. Who is going to be for it?

But some key issues remained for Welch, as for all leaders of organizations who aspire to run flat operations where excess layers of management are removed and where bureaucratic behavior is replaced by boundaryless behavior.

To start, the presence of a flat organization is often in the eye of the beholder, and the worst person in the organization to assess its flatness can be the CEO. I have observed dozens of companies and other groups (and even worked in a few) where the top leaders congratulated themselves for running flat operations with minimal bureaucracy. But outside the handful of officers clustered around the executive suite, few employees felt it or believed it.

Some leaders believe that picking up the phone and calling employees directly at lower levels of the hierarchy without going through layers of superiors means they run flat and open operations. But that's hardly a realistic test—the top gun can always call on anybody, right down to the janitor. The true test is, can those lower-level people pick up the phone and call the CEO—and can they do so without intimidation from either the CEO or (more likely) their intermediary superiors?

Even in a company where the openness really does flow in both directions, another hurdle to successfully instilling and capitalizing on a boundaryless culture remains. It is much easier for the CEO than for anyone else to operate successfully in such an environment and enjoy doing so. That's because the CEO has a vastly superior array of resources to call upon to study, implement, and follow up on new initiatives and ideas.

The CEO can usually turn to a sizable personal staff and budget and veer from the prearranged course and program of work with impunity. And if such activities don't pan out? Aside from the really big blunders, they can usually be made to disappear with few traces or recriminations. Conditions are decidedly different for underlings, who haven't nearly the same level of flexibility, resources, freedom to act, and personal motivation to behave in such a fashion.

DOES WELCH WALK THE WALK?

HOW DID JACK WELCH personally try to walk the walk and not just talk the talk when it came to smashing the bureaucracy, erasing the boundaries, and ensuring that his entire organization—and not only himself—got to operate in a non-bureaucratic climate?

One key tool was the thousands of "Work-Out" sessions held with employees at all levels. Specific bureaucracy-busting ideas often bubbled up from these meetings. Without them, managers would never have been able to get a handle on what the bureaucracy really means to the average employee.

Then there were the more than 250 times Welch has personally appeared in "the Pit" at the GE training center at Crotonville, New York. I'll return to the topic in Chapter 8, but it's clear that standing before some 15,000 company managers and interacting directly with them on company practices and procedures further enabled Welch to realistically assess the level of bureaucracy rather than simply believing his own rhetoric on the subject.

Also important was the informality Welch attempted to instill at GE. He regarded this as more than just the trappings of style—it was a critical management strategy as well. "The story about GE that hasn't been told is the value of an informal place," he told *Business Week* in 1998. "I think it's a big thought. I don't think that people have ever figured out that being informal is a big deal."[13]

What specifically did this mean to GE under Welch? "Everyone, from secretaries to chauffeurs to factory workers, calls him Jack," explained *Business Week*. "Everyone can expect—at one time or another—to see him scurry down an aisle to pick through the merchandise on a bottom shelf or to reach into his pocket and surprise with an unexpected bonus."[14] Like former President George Bush, Welch was famous for his countless handwritten notes, often transmitted via fax, to thousands of company employees at many levels in the organization. He was said to know at least a thousand people at GE by sight, remembering their names and jobs when they met in the hall.

But to Welch, instilling an atmosphere of informality went beyond even those manifestations. "Informality in GE means so much more than calling people by their first names or the absence of managers' suits and ties or reserved parking spaces and other trappings of rank," he explained recently.[15]

"Informality means that anyone anywhere in the company with a good idea, a new view, feels empowered—and, in fact, expected—to deliver it to anyone else and know it'll be listened to and valued."[16]

MEET THE NEW BOSS— SAME AS THE OLD BOSS

CREATING A DELAYERED, boundaryless organization that shuns bureaucracy in favor of speed, simplicity, and self-confidence is an undeniably appealing and meritorious concept. But another issue leaders must face as they strive for it is to ensure that they don't replace the old bureaucracy with a new bureaucracy.

Who would that bureaucracy include? Most likely the CEO and the inner circle—doing precisely the kind of meddling and micromanaging they tried to get rid of by eliminating layers of bureaucrats.

The goal is a management approach akin to the technique jockey Willie Shoemaker said he used to win races—a light touch on the horse's reins. "The horse never knows I'm there until he needs me," Willie said. But how many hard-charging chief executives can resist the temptation to look over everyone's shoulders, especially if they've rid the organization of some of those who used to perform that function?

In Welch's case, his degree of involvement often depended on his estimation of a manager's performance and abilities. "If you're doing well, you probably have more freedom than most CEOs of publicly traded companies," remarked one GE executive to *Business Week* in 1998. "But the leash gets pulled very tightly when a unit is underperforming."[17]

Welch appeared sensitive to the possibility that the benefits of creating a boundaryless organization could end up being undercut by the CEO himself. And he articulated a rather unorthodox theory to deal with the problem: "overextended" leaders—people overextended by the number of direct reports they have to deal with—wind up being the best leaders.

Why? "Because they don't have time to meddle and because they create under them people who by necessity have to take on more responsibility."[18] In Welch's estimation, giving a leader more direct reports not only flattens the organization and gratifies more people through personal access to the top, it keeps that leader very, very busy. The less idle the hands, the less meddling mischief they can create!

IS BUREAUCRACY NECESSARY?

EVERYONE LOVES TO hate bureaucrats, but in reality many bureaucracies are there for a reason—to provide services, to keep needed records, and to police behavior and ensure that everyone plays by the rules. (And believe me, I hated to say that as much as you probably hated to read it!)

In the case of a massive organization like a giant corporation, a government, an army, or a medical provider, isn't a reasonable level of bureaucracy necessary to standardize certain practices and exercise a needed level of oversight over the behavior of fallible human beings?

Some observers have suggested that General Electric had to learn this lesson the hard way in several instances before and during the tenure of Jack Welch. For example, when the company was hit with 20 indictments for illegal price fixing from 1959 to 1961—with three executives doing jail time—GE developed and implemented a strict code of conduct.

Can the competitive, results-oriented ethic of GE, combined with a delayered and decentralized culture, lead to both the cutting of corners and the failure to detect such conduct when it is happening? A few critics suggested this was the case when the scandal involving GE-owned Kidder Peabody broke.

General Electric bought the brokerage firm in 1986 for $602 million. Before there were any real signs of return on the investment, GE had reportedly pumped up to $1 billion into its acquisition. Then in 1994 it was discovered that a young Kidder Peabody trader named Joseph Jett had created some $350 million in phantom profits to inflate his own bonuses.

The scandal rocked Wall Street and was seen as placing a sizable chink in Jack Welch's armor. The *Wall Street Journal* reported that a "chorus of second-guessers . . . is asking whether Mr. Welch . . . has cut the bureaucracy and decentralized GE so much as to have paved the way for the Kidder fiasco." The report went on to quote a Harvard Business School professor who suggested Welch "has built a culture of individual fiefdoms and that decentralized responsibility leaves a firm like GE vulnerable."[19]

GE advocates countered that the company's internal audit functions had been greatly strengthened and that its financial dealings were among the most tightly controlled of any large corporation.

Welch's response eventually included firing long-time friend Michael A. Carpenter, who was in charge of Kidder, and selling the remaining remnants of the firm to Paine Webber in exchange for a 23-percent stake in that company. The irony is that the booming stock market of 1990s significantly boosted the value of those shares, turning the Kidder Peabody lemon into lemonade for Jack Welch and GE.

SHARED VALUES ARE MORE EFFECTIVE THAN IMPOSED RULES

THE LESSON THAT GE's leader took from the brokerage house scandal was not to backpedal on his attack on bureaucracy—far from it. Instead Welch stepped up efforts to persuade, motivate, and inspire employees in his boundaryless organization to embrace the distinctive blend of values he believed would make General Electric a distinctively successful and decent global company in the 21st century. The mid-1990s saw a heightened focus on the importance of integrity in this values mix and the inclusion of values as well as bottom-line results in the criteria GE used to hire, fire, promote, and pay its executives.

"In the early 1990s," Welch wrote in 1998, "after we had finished defining ourselves as a company of boundaryless people with a thirst for learning and a compulsion to share, it became unthinkable for us to tolerate—much less hire or promote—the tyrant, the turf defender, the autocrat, the big shot.

"They were simply 'yesterday.'"[20]

WELCH ON LEADERSHIP:
BEATING THE BUREAUCRACY

- Leaders must fight bureaucracy in their organizations at every turn—but at the same time keep enough structure in place to control expenditures, monitor results, and detect wayward behavior.

- Successful leaders must smash through barriers that prevent the free exchange of ideas. "Command and control" management approaches don't work in today's Internet economy.

- Leaders at the top should not assume they run "flat" organizations simply because they have decreed it. Their perception is often radically different than that of employees down the line who may find themselves under the thumb of an oppressive midlevel manager.

- Organizations that are overly reliant on process, control, paperwork, reporting requirements, and chains of command are in Jack Welch's words, "dead ducks."

CHAPTER 8

PEOPLE POWER

＊

No man will make a great leader who wants to do it all himself, or to get all the credit for doing it.
—ANDREW CARNEGIE

THROUGH MOST OF the 1980s, Jack Welch engineered a process of "creative destruction" at General Electric. Externally, that meant the sale of dozens of businesses and the acquisition of dozens more to make the company more global and service oriented. Internally it meant shedding tens of thousands of workers and wiping out entire layers of middle management in a frontal assault on the company's massive bureaucracy. It was "creative" in the sense that there was a purpose behind it, a strategy to it, and an overall positive result planned for it.

Each of these moves, as painful as many of them were, was designed to help the company compete in the new era of globalization, deregulation, and information technology that was rapidly emerging. To survive and prosper in such an era, Welch strongly believed, GE had to remain big and diverse in its mix of businesses—while at the same time making decisions, grabbing opportunities, engineering innovations, and caring for customers in the same way that America's best smaller companies were doing.

Much of Welch's public image as well as his legacy as a leader can be found as a result of those early moves:

The readiness to stand up to the conventional wisdom, to make tough decisions and stick with them in the face of strong personal attacks

Leaping for the big deal, shunning the incremental, and rendering quick decisions with a yes or a no but almost never a maybe

Dispensing with the formalities and many of the pretensions of the corporate world and replacing dispassionate analysis with a passionate search for bold ideas

The insistence that GE businesses be number one or number two in their markets or be fixed, sold, or closed—underscoring that if you worked at GE it was results that counted

The relentless focus on shareholder value and the judgment of the marketplace, even if it meant massive layoffs and selling pieces of GE's history—on the theory that in the new environment, a company without investor confidence would fail and you'd soon be forced to do it anyway

A love of change and a loathing of bureaucracy

These leadership values, combined with Welch's business strategies, served GE well in the 1980s. But after blasting through the thick walls of the company's ossified bureaucracy, dumping losing businesses, and throwing process and convention out the window, Welch still had a company to run. After tearing down the house he found when becoming chairman, he had to establish what kind of house he wanted to erect in its place. He faced the question of whether his principal legacy at GE be to overthrow the old order or to be a builder of a new one.

Welch understood his challenge early on. Early in the 1990s he said: "The biggest mistake we could make right now is to think that simply doing more of what worked in the '80s will be enough to win in the '90s. It won't."[1]

He saw the moves of the 1980s as the structural revolution. It was focused on competing with the Japanese and the Germans. It emphasized getting "lean and mean" and moving faster. It dealt with the hardware of the company—which businesses belonged in the mix and which didn't? How much staff was needed to run the ones that remained? What processes were necessary to ensure product and service quality? Which ones represented needless and foolish bureaucracy?

Dealing with these issues restored momentum to GE's earnings growth and won Welch plaudits on Wall Street and throughout the business world. From a personal standpoint he probably could have coasted on that momentum and lived off that reputation for years to come. But he had other ideas.

A new revolution would be needed to maintain the company's upward trajectory. If the 1980s revolution was a structural one, mostly about hardware, the 1990s revolution was cultural; it was all about people. The first was designed to make the company more competitive; the second, to make the company more productive. Welch saw that as the new battleground for business in the 1990s and beyond.

Some critics found the notion that the man they called "Neutron Jack"—the CEO who had been named the "toughest boss in America"—was now a "people person" setting out to nurture and empower every lowly employee ironic or even laughable. Others saw it as a ploy to reshape his public image on the theory that everyone, even a guy like Jack Welch, wants to be approved of and liked.

Yet it was a logical next step for the GE chairman. In hindsight Welch's second revolution looks remarkably prescient. The 1990s was when mankind developed and widely disseminated its most useful and enhancing tools since the discovery of fire or the invention of the wheel, the printing press, and the internal combustion engine—the personal computer and Internet communications.

These tools were both empowering and demanding. Empowering because they exponentially multiplied the capabilities of the individual, made it much harder for bosses or governments to keep secrets from that individual, and increased the opportunities for all employees to live and work on their own terms. But the tools were also demanding. They required new kinds of knowledge workers and made it necessary for them to continually upgrade their skills. Successful employees—productive employees—would have to be in a learning environment over an entire career.

Jack Welch came relatively late to the high-tech and Internet party. In a way, that was fortunate; he missed out on the short-lived era in which many forgot that the Internet and computer technologies were after all only tools—means to an end, not ends in and of themselves. It's people—well-trained and ready to be continually retrained, energetic, motivated, passionate about what they do—who really matter.

And yet as the mature economies of the West and Japan head into the 21st century, another fundamental development makes Jack Welch's focus on human talent right on target— relatively speaking there's going to be less of it available. People are living longer and having relatively fewer children. The United States will still grow in population due to immigration and high birth rates among some communities, but it will be more modest growth than in earlier times—particularly among those of working age. In a nation like Japan the population will actually start to drop within 20 to 30 years.

What this means for business is an increasingly intense competition for workers at all skill levels. Companies are going to have to work hard to attract the best and the brightest, appealing to them not only in terms of salary and benefits but on values, sense of mission, and opportunities for personal achievement and fulfillment.

Jack Welch's second revolution is geared to winning this competition, which is a more problematic and considerably tougher competition than the one GE faced in the 1980s. To win the competition for the best employees. To win the competition for the most productive workforce. To make General Electric an open, freewheeling learning environment where each individual feels part of a greater cause but at the same time finds in the company a vehicle for personal attainment. "People want the chance to do their own thing, to grow, to flourish, to reach their dreams," he has said. "It's all about trust, it's not about you telling them what to do. You still have to hire the very best brains in the world, work hard, motivate them, pay them.

"As long as you get the best people, let them go, always have someone better than you, it works. It really works."[2]

WORK-OUT

WHAT ARE THE PILLARS of Jack Welch's cultural revolution at GE? The revolution was meant to unleash a torrent of higher productivity and creativity and thus earnings and growth by attracting the best human talent in the world and molding them into leaders. How did it work?

It started with Work-Out. From its beginning in March 1989, the Work-Out program has consisted of an ongoing series of company retreats, normally three days in length, each involving approximately 50 employees of varying rank and responsibility. A senior executive sets the tone and goals, then leaves the session while participants discuss company processes and make suggestions for improving products and services while eliminating wasteful practices. On appropriate occasions, customers, suppliers, and business partners are included in the Work-Out.

Attendees are encouraged to argue with and criticize superiors. Those superiors, including the top manager (who returns toward the end of the process), are required to respond immediately to proposals generated by the group. For the most part decisions are made on the spot—yes or no. Maybes are allowed only when the matter under consideration is particularly complex.

Welch and a top lieutenant conceived of the Work-Out program after returning from one of the CEO's frequent sessions in "the Pit" at GE's management development and training center at Crotonville, New York. Welch was reflecting, with considerable satisfaction, on the group that joined him in the auditorium that day—about 150 feisty and argumentative senior managers who fought with him and challenged him throughout his presentation.

That was the goal of those sessions. Welch believed he learned a lot from them and that they made GE's up-and-coming executives feel they could have direct access to the boss. Well, if it made sense for some, why not for all? Welch set about to institutionalize the format on a company-wide basis.

It was tagged Work-Out because the company at the time was in the process of installing fitness centers at many facilities so employees could exercise, get in shape, and in the process feel energized and interact with others they might not otherwise get to know. The parallels clearly intrigued Welch, a workout buff of many years' standing.

"Work-Out is based on the simple belief that people closest to the work know more than anyone how it can be done better," Welch told shareholders in his 1995 letter. "It was this enormous reservoir of untapped knowledge, and insight, that we wanted to draw upon."[3]

On one level Welch was enticed by the potential for cost savings and product improvements. Work-Out participants started "clear-cutting" with a vengeance. "The idea is to challenge every single piece of conventional wisdom," explained the executive who helped Welch create the program. "Everything is guilty until proven innocent."[4] Confirms one early participant: "We just basically took out pens and paper and started crossing out things. . . . We removed the work that was meaningless."[5]

Here are some examples from various Work-Out sessions:

GE welders won permission to select their own tools and machines instead of having white-collar managers, who didn't use the tools or machines, do it for them.

An editor received authority to issue her company newsletter with only one approval instead of several.

The X-ray unit of GE Medical Systems generated 55 items to be eliminated or improved.

The firm's financial department learned that 1,000 employees worked nights and weekends so GE could be first to get its quarterly earnings report to Wall Street. Welch's reaction: "Who the heck cares about reporting first? Maybe somebody did, once. Or maybe somebody thought someone did." The make-work practice was eliminated.

A silicone plastics lab was virtually redesigned.

NBC Sports shaved $1 million off the costs of televising professional football games.[6]

Within two years of the program's inauguration, approximately 1,000 Work-Out sessions were convened. By 1996 almost all employees had participated, with as many as 20,000 members of GE's workforce involved on a single day.[7] Welch had come a long way toward his stated goal of making Work-Outs "as natural an act as coming to work."[8]

"At workouts, people who often have no occasion to speak to one another during the day—hourly workers, salaried managers and union leaders—are summoned to the corporate equivalent of a New England town meeting," the *Economist* summed up in a 1991 report. "The pioneering workouts quickly developed into savage attacks on the worst examples of corporate bureaucracy—ten signatures on a minor requisition, artificial dress codes."[9]

Indeed, in addition to the money GE saved and products and processes it improved, no doubt Welch derived a visceral satisfaction from the argumentative culture Work-Outs spawned, especially when directed against the hated bureaucracy. A challenging man by nature, Welch thrives in a climate of verbal combat and quick-witted repartee. Ideas should be able to withstand vigorous argument. If not, there's probably something wrong with them.

"Constructive conflict" is what he called it. Welch "brought a much more freewheeling, entrepreneurial style to GE, in which shouting is welcomed and arguments encouraged," the *Los Angeles Times* reported even before the Work-Out program had begun.[10]

Most important to Welch, however, was the empowering quality of the Work-Out sessions. They helped him meet the challenge to "involve everyone—to spread our new openness into every corner of our Company, to give every one of our . . . employees what the best small companies give: voice."[11]

Assessing the impact, Welch credited Work-Out with being an effective vehicle to achieve his oft-stated goal of creating a boundaryless organization that moved in the marketplace with speed, simplicity, and self-confidence. "After a decade of Work-Out, most of the old bureaucracy and the boundaries among us have been demolished," he told shareholders in his 1997 missive. "Finding the better way, the best idea, from whoever will share it with us, has become our central focus."[12]

Welch was keen on eliminating the Not Invented Here syndrome, which he believed pushed GE into arrogance and complacency. Work-Out went after that problem too, Welch believed, and as a by-product prompted other changes that were in keeping with the spirit of sharing the best ideas and accepting them from anyone. "We made major changes in the compensation program to support this learning behavior," Welch reported. "Before Work-Out we operated under a management philosophy that rewarded 'original' ideas and 'standout' performances."

Not anymore. Today the company "rewards the finding and sharing of ideas even more than their origination."[13]

The institutionalization of the Work-Out program at General Electric is a testament to Welch's vision, but just as important, to his understanding that leadership is much more than coming up with nice phrases, making a couple speeches, holding up a few positive examples, and walking away. Leadership means taking that vision and spreading it around with passion throughout every level of an organization. It's about preaching the message again and again and again, refreshing it regularly, and holding people's feet to the fire until they get with the program.

Warmly as it was received inside and outside GE, Work-Out still evokes skepticism because it runs smack into some basic habits of human nature. Few people really enjoy living in a combative, critical environment where face-to-face argument and contention dominate. Circumspection, keeping your opinions to yourself (especially when dealing with superiors and peers), seems like the safer and frankly, the nicer, course. Work-Out observers have in fact reported that many participants were timid in the meetings. Others were distrustful. Despite the company's promise of no retribution for their comments, they clearly wondered what subtle resentments would breed inside the mind of a boss they publicly challenged.

I have participated in Work-Out-like sessions at a couple of organizations. I enjoy them because—like Welch—I find verbal combat over programs and ideas exciting. Others do not; they sit silent in such meetings. Are they dumb? Are they gutless? Are they devoid of ideas? No. It's simply not an environment in which they are comfortable or proficient.

Another conclusion I have drawn from my own participation in such sessions and my observations of the CEO and corporate cultures is that the top boss (at least usually) is the easiest target for criticism in this day and age. It's become a kind of management ritual, thanks in large part to Jack Welch, for CEOs to invite criticism as a way to show their openness and self-confidence. They're paid to take the guff. It's a badge of honor for those who take it and those who give it.

Much more difficult and rare is criticism of peers. In the Work-Out-style retreats I have attended, the back-and-forth with the CEO lived up to its billing, but when it came time for, say, one vice president to critique a program or approach of another, everyone clammed up. On one occasion I asked a colleague why he didn't question or respond to a peer's report, when that colleague had repeatedly been highly critical of his peer in private?

He looked at me wide-eyed and said, "Oh I would *never* burn a colleague like that—not in front of everyone and especially not in front of the boss." But that didn't stop him from resuming his water-cooler griping back in the office.

Thus Work-Outs are undoubtedly successful at removing vertical boundaries between bosses and their direct reports, but in my experience their effectiveness at removing horizontal boundaries—encouraging each person to freely critique and contribute to the group of peers—falls short.

SIX SIGMA

THE SECOND PILLAR of Jack Welch's cultural revolution at GE was his quality control initiative, Six Sigma. Developed at smaller companies and perfected at two large ones,

Motorola and AlliedSignal, Six Sigma is a specific methodology designed to slash the number of defects in a company's
end-to-end process of producing, improving selling, distribut-
ing, and servicing its products. A company the size of General
Electric, operating at a "brass ring" Six Sigma level (specifically, fewer than 3.4 defects per million operations in a manufacturing or service process), could save billions of dollars
per year.

Welch sees Work-Out and Six Sigma as complementary
but distinct programs. Both are meant to spur a continuous
process of improvement and to bind disparate GE businesses
and employees together with a common language and a common cause.

"Just as Work-Out got us to a culture of learning and
openness that defined the way we behave, quality improvement under the disciplined rubric of Six Sigma methodology
will define the way we work," he told shareholders in his 1996
letter.[14] In an important sense, Six Sigma represents a matura-
tion of Welch's "people power" initiatives at GE. Starting
from the useful but unruly bull and gripe corporate therapy
sessions of Work-Out, Welch tried to channel that teamwork
and energy into a more disciplined process that could produce
systemic changes and improvements in company processes
and even new breakthroughs in products and services offered
to customers.

Six Sigma was inaugurated at the company in late 1995
with 200 projects. It grew to 6,000 by 1997. By the time of his
farewell annual meeting address in 2001, Welch was prepared
to declare that "originally focused on reducing waste and elevating the quality of our products and processes within the
Company, it has delivered billions of dollars to GE's bottom

line in savings." Welch cited several examples of Six Sigma improvements:

Medical Systems improved the life of CT scanner X-ray tubes by a factor of ten.

Superabrasives—GE's industrial diamond business—was able to quadruple return on investment.

The railcar leasing business achieved a 62 percent reduction in repair shop turnaround time.[15]

But ultimately Welch saw the greatest contributions of Six Sigma taking place in the facilities of the company's customers. The initiative took on an outside focus, he reported, on "improving the productivity and efficiency of our customers' operations. Six Sigma increased the intimacy between GE and its customer base." Among the examples he marveled at in his 2001 speech to share owners:

GE Medical Systems undertook more than 1,000 projects at customer hospitals, giving clients $100 million in benefits.

GE's Aircraft Engines business saved airline customers $320 million.

By focusing Six Sigma benefits on customers, Welch attempted the ultimate act of business boundarylessness—erasing the lines between company and customer. By expanding the straightforward buy, sell, and service equation into an ongoing series of creative interactions with customers, GE hopes to forge the strongest possible bonds with them.

"If GE's destiny is to become the greatest company of the 21st century," Welch said, "we must be the world's most customer focused company as well."[16]

Some have suggested that Six Sigma—with its elaborate methodologies and systems, which at GE have required the training of thousands of employees divided into rankings of "Master Black Belts," "Black Belts," and "Green Belts"—has the potential to reinstitute bureaucracy at the company under a different guise.

Welch didn't share those concerns, instead enthusiastically proclaiming that Six Sigma "has spread like wildfire across the Company, and it is transforming everything we do."[17] In his 2001 annual meeting speech he referred to "zealot after zealot" reporting positive results from Six Sigma projects. (*Zealot* is obviously a complimentary term in the Welch lexicon, at least as it relates to General Electric!) He has made it clear that proficiency in the methodology will be part of the job requirement for future company leaders. You might think he'd have difficulty enforcing this requirement from his retirement, but don't worry: "Six Sigma is quickly becoming part of the genetic code" of General Electric.[18]

Like Work-Out, Six Sigma showcases the need for the successful leader to craft a compelling vision and work doggedly with passion and energy to spread it around the culture of the organization. Yet as important as this is in motivating and rallying all participants to contribute to the mission, most of us are going to look first and foremost at how we and others are individually rewarded—or punished—for our efforts.

That brings me to the next pillar of Welch's cultural revolution at General Electric—and the next chapter.

WELCH ON LEADERSHIP:
EMPOWERING PEOPLE

- In an era of services and technology, people represent the leader's most important asset.

- With changing demographics (the aging of the population and declining birth rates) organizations must compete fiercely for the best human talent. It is often the quality and style of leadership that determines who will win that competition and where the best people will want to work.

- Creating an environment where every person feels free to contribute and is motivated to put in extra effort is no simple task. Jack Welch spent years devising the mechanisms, such as Work-Out and Six Sigma, to create this climate at GE.

- Arguments and debates should be encouraged, as long as they are conducted with respect. Creative conflict produces better ideas and exposes weak ones. Bringing disagreements out in the open reduces hallway gossip sessions and water-cooler whispering.

- Leaders must set the tone at the top and make a personal commitment to fostering an inclusive environment. Simply declaring it as an organization policy is not enough.

- Successful leaders are not afraid to surround themselves with strong-willed, capable people—doing so makes them successful!

CHAPTER 9

FROM BUREAUCRACY
TO MERITOCRACY

———————

This is all about meritocracy. This isn't socialism.
—JACK WELCH, 2000[1]

You can talk—you can preach—about "a learning company," but . . .
reinforcing management appraisal and compensation systems is critical.[2]
—JACK WELCH, 1997

IN A PROFESSIONAL WORLD of stultifying sameness—
where employees in companies, governments, educational institutions, and other organizations often receive useless pro
forma evaluations and the same virtually automatic (and usually small) raises regardless of performance—Jack Welch's
GE was different. Through his actions, Welch demonstrated
that a major test of leadership and a fundamental requirement for achieving excellence, productivity, and growth is to
replace the dull expectations of bureaucracy with the rewards
and opportunities of meritocracy. That means treating no two
people the same and rewarding individuals according to their
performance and their values—even when the result is a vastly
uneven system of raises and promotions—opening the com-

pany to charges of unfairness and favoritism, and even to workplace lawsuits.

Replacing GE's bureaucracy with a meritocracy founded on performance and values was another critical pillar of Welch's cultural revolution, offering many insights on his leadership.

Leadership is all about making decisions with speed, conviction, and courage—and no area of endeavor tests leaders' mettle more than the decisions related to the people they have been charged with managing and guiding. Human nature prompts most of us to avoid confrontations and unpleasant situations, to tell people what they want to hear, to define fairness by treating everyone the same, and to take the easy way out by punting on harsh judgments. In the organizational setting, these impulses lead managers to delay and duck decisions like firing those who don't pull their weight. They tempt executives to duck responsibility by paying and promoting the mediocre staffer the same as the stellar performer.

In the abstract, it's easy to understand the folly of such a course. It's price goes far beyond the cost of dead-weight employees—you dissipate the spirit and squander the energy of the best workers, eventually driving many of them away and doing incalculable damage to the organization in an era where human talent is everything.

But understanding that reality and coming up with the systems, the discipline, and the guts required to create and sustain a meritocracy of human talent are two different things. The task is further complicated by the danger that even if you decide to pursue the winning course toward meritocracy, your implementation may be flawed. The leader must exercise enormous judgment in the process of differentiating among employees, taking care to reward workers on true merit and not according to snap judgments, favoritism, cronyism, or who does the best job of sucking up to the boss.

Jack Welch's conviction that the fair and empowering approach is to pay and promote people differently rather than similarly started early in his life. As noted earlier, he was appalled when, after his first year on the job at GE, he got the same raise as others he thought he had outperformed. Welch actually handed in his resignation and accepted a position at a company he believed would pay him what he was worth. It took a last-minute appeal, along with a better raise and a promotion, to convince him to abort his plan to leave.

This personal lesson was not lost on Welch once he assumed the chairmanship of the company. Dealing with employee issues—from the massive layoffs of the early 1980s to the overhaul of GE's evaluation and pay system later in the decade to the redefinition of what it meant to be a star player at the company in the 1990s—was a major preoccupation of his tenure.

THE FEAR OF LETTING GO

WELCH, OF COURSE, came to fame in the business world by launching substantial rounds of layoffs and middle management cutbacks at General Electric. These firings "traumatized a company that traditionally gave its employees an implicit job-for-life promise," reported the *Economist* in 1991. "And it has earned Mr. Welch a reputation for arrogance and ruthlessness that he finds embarrassing."[3]

For his part, Welch reasonably insisted that lifetime job pledges made by companies that were not productive, competitive, innovative, or growing were really false promises. Calling his approach to staffing "hard-headed but warmhearted," he pointed to a range of severance benefits and job-training and placement services designed to make an employee's journey out of GE as smooth as possible.

Indeed, the manner in which organizations deal with employee dismissals can be as important as the fact that they have decided they must fire people in the first place. Human resource experts have devised all sorts of theories about the best way to perform the unpleasant task (don't let people go right before Christmas, make sure no one gets a layoff notice as a birthday present, and so on). But as the bonds of company-employee loyalty have frayed over recent years, the process has also been complicated by concerns that a worker on the way out may sabotage or steal before leaving—or worse, march in the next day with a gun.

As a result, cruelly executed firings still frequently occur. I have known several employees at different organizations who reported to work faithfully or years, only to be told they were being laid off. Security and human resources people stood over their shoulders while they cleaned out their desks and then escorted them out of the building. No matter what justifications or theories are spun around that kind of treatment, the bottom line is, it still stinks.

Only the sadistic boss is pleased by the painful process of dismissing employees, and it takes a cold mind to be left unmoved by it. The far more common response is to duck the issue. Many executives talk tough about getting rid of underperformers, but then leave them in place. Or if they do act, they stay holed up in their offices while sending their lieu-tenants in to do the dirty work.

Removing someone against their will from the ranks of an organization is one of the toughest tests for a leader—and it is all the tougher when the reason for the firing is not the company's need to trim the fat but the employee's inadequacies. In those cases, there is no company-wide layoff plan or bad business climate to hide behind. Can the leader look someone in the eye and deliver necessary bad news? Can the leader face up to the consequences of the decision, even when it results in an emotional confrontation with an underling?

Welch is one leader who has. "Jack can be tough as nails . . . on business results, on people assessments," a GE human relations executive confirmed recently. "We remove 10 to 15 percent of our executives on an annual basis for non-performance. Most corporations don't do that."[4]

Still Welch wanted to make sure people know he didn't really enjoy the weeding-out process. "My reputation for harshness is overblown," he said. "From the beginning it has been stamped on my forehead, though to a certain extent it is understandable. I made changes that upset people's lives. They'd like someone to blame."[5]

As for those dismissed because they couldn't perform, Welch believes "the cruelest thing any organization can do is not level with people. Then, too often, it's too late in careers."[6]

Welch's maxims about letting people go are familiar ones in corporate America. If you do not fit in at the company, if you cannot meet performance expectations, or if your job can no longer be sustained or justified due to business conditions, it is better for all to acknowledge the reality up front, move out, and move on. The sooner you get settled at a new organization or in a new career, the better it will be for your family, your finances, and your personal development.

Understandably, many departing employees (and those who fear they could be next on the chopping block) hear these ideas in different terms. "I'm doing you a favor by firing you. You should thank me" is the bitter and only message they hear being delivered by the boss.

It's part of the price and responsibility of leadership.

MAKING THE GRADE

LESS GUT-WRENCHING than firing people is another set of decisions that many executives and managers also prefer to ignore and duck—evaluating employees and paying or penalizing them according to those evaluations.

Most of us who have ever managed have learned to loathe filling out those dreaded reviews. Our frustrations are exacerbated if we have systems in place that are almost certainly going to pay and promote people the same anyway. Predetermined even-handedness undercuts the integrity and the spirit of the evaluation process, turning the exercise into a waste of time and rendering it all but useless.

Did Welch institute an honest process of evaluating and paying his managers—or was he just talking a good game?

According to company executives and observers, Welch indeed "walked the talk." Early on he overhauled the way GE evaluated and paid (or penalized) employees. "There's a new degree of candor," in measuring performance, reported one GE official back in 1987. Liberal uses of bonuses encouraged top performers and were meant to spur lesser achievers onward. One year during the 1980s at GE Appliances, for example, 25 percent of the managers got bonuses averaging $1,400 with the checks handed out right on the shop floor.[7]

By the end of Welch's tenure, yearly raises at GE sometimes ran as high as 25 percent even when the average was 4 percent and there was no promotion involved. It was not unusual for cash bonuses to add up to 20 to 70 percent of a good performer's base pay.

Another device used to great effect by Welch was the expansion of stock options from a small handful of top executives—400 when he started—to more than 22,000 employees at all levels of the company by 1995. Doing so "aligns the interests of the individual, the company and the share owner behind powerful one-company results," he explained in his 1995 Letter to Share Owners.[8]

By 1998, 27,000 GE employees had stock options, with 1,200 holding options worth over a million dollars. GE pay, bonus, and stock option incentives meant "that everyone is getting the rewards, not just a few of us. That's a big deal," Welch enthused to *Business Week*. "We're changing their game and their lives. They've got their kids' tuition or they've got a second house. That's a real kick. We've all got plenty. We're fat cats."[9]

Welch's commitment to the time and toil it takes to measure results, assess performance, and communicate judgments and guidance was demonstrated by the amount of personal time he devoted to the process. Each year he went out into the field to review GE's major businesses. He kept close tabs on the records of approximately 500 top executives and he personally wrote lengthy regular reviews of his senior leadership team. The core of his approach was "differentiation" in the doling out or denial of pay and promotion. In Welch view, that's how people are motivated and even though it takes more time and trouble and generates more controversy, it's a leader's responsibility to make the tough, discerning judgments. "Welch skillfully uses rewards to drive behavior," noted *Business Week* in 1998, and he always demanded that they be highly differentiated. "I can't stand nondifferential stuff," the CEO confirmed. "We live in differentiation."[10]

Other executives at the company found they'd better be prepared to follow his example. That's why he called them *leaders,* not managers. "Call people managers and they are going to start managing things, getting in the way," he told *Fortune.* "The job of a leader is to take the available resources—human and financial—and allocate them rigorously. Not to spread them out evenly like butter on bread. That's what bureaucrats do."[11]

CHOOSING AMONG UNEQUALS: THE "A" PLAYERS

WITH DIFFERENTIATION among GE's professional ranks deemed so essential, how did Jack Welch look at his workforce and determine who to reward for performance, coach to improve, or send on their way to new careers elsewhere?

"We break our population down into three categories: the top 20 percent, the valuable high performance 70 percent, and the bottom 10 percent," Welch explained. His GE did a lot to pay, promote, and retain the top tier, and tried to improve and encourage the vast swath of middle performers. As for those at the bottom, GE managers had to have "the determination to change out, always humanely, that bottom 10 percent and do it every single year. That's how real meritocracies are created and thrive."[12]

The top performers—"A" players, Welch called them—got the lion's share of inducements, with great efforts made to ensure they were constantly "rewarded in the soul and wallet." Why? "Because they are the ones who make magic happen. Losing one of these people must be held up as a leadership sin." Indeed executives higher up the food chain were judged heavily on their ability to keep the most promising talent at GE.[13]

Executives were also judged strictly in their disposition of the bottom 10 percent of underachievers. Not firing them was regarded as "not only a management failure but false kindness as well—a form of cruelty."[14]

How did the GE chairman define an "A" player? "A man or woman with a vision and the ability to articulate that vision to the team, so vividly and so powerfully that it also becomes their vision." These stars must also have the "courage to make the tough call—decisively but with fairness and absolute integrity."[15]

Over time, Welch believed, GE would repopulate itself with this kind of executive. "As we go forward there will be nothing but 'A's' in every leadership position in this Company."[16]

WHEN PERFORMANCE ISN'T ENOUGH: WHY "TYPE IV" LEADERS MUST GO

CLEARLY, THOUGH, the most talked about and unorthodox credo of the Jack Welch meritocracy was his division of the GE leadership class into four distinct categories, and the earmarking of one group for removal despite good financial performance.

He began to make this distinction when various Work-Out sessions revealed that "some of the rhetoric heard at the corporate level . . . did not match the reality of life in the businesses. The problem was that some of our leaders were unwilling, or unable, to abandon big-company, big-shot autocracy and embrace the values we were trying to grow."[17] From that rather unsurprising discovery, Welch went on to delineate four management types, assessing how each furthered or blocked the values of openness, sharing, informality, and boundaryless behavior.

- Type I: "Not only delivers on performance commitments but believes in and furthers GE's small company values." These are the "A" players who "will represent the core of our senior leadership into the next Century."

- Type II: "Does not meet our commitments, nor share our values—nor last long at GE."

- Type III: "Believes in the values but sometimes misses the commitments." These managers are usually coached, encouraged, and given another chance.

- Type IV: Those who make their numbers but don't share the values. Making the call on these managers is the most difficult of all, Welch says. They deliver on the results "but they do it while ignoring values." They are a destructive force because they poison the atmosphere, wear people down, stifle creativity, and cause valuable talent down the line to flee GE.[18]

General Norman Schwarzkopf has defined leadership as "a combination of strategy and character. If you must be without one, be without the strategy." Welch employed similar reasoning when he made what he called a "watershed decision" to rid the company of Type IV managers. Their short-term business strategies might be proven and successful but they lacked the ability to conform to the kind of character, culture, and values he believed necessary for GE's continued prosperity.

"The manager who makes the numbers but who doesn't have the values, who is the go-to person, the hard-ass, the driver," must be discarded, Welch insisted, because even though the company benefited in the short term, it would lose significantly over the longer haul. The highest price to be paid for keeping Type IV managers is that you drive away human talent, which Welch regarded as the whole ball game for companies in the 21st century. "You lose people until you move them out," he explains.[19]

For a man who has been singularly focused on "making his numbers" for Wall Street, deciding to base major management hiring and firing decisions on the way executives conduct themselves and treat people as well as performance was indeed a watershed decision. So intent was Welch on proving that GE was "walking the talk" when it came to creating a learning company that he even prescribed an approach to removing Type IVs that conjured up the image of public hangings in the days of the Wild West. In his 2000 Letter to Share Owners he wrote:

> We began removing Type IV managers and made it clear to the entire Company why they were being asked to leave . . . not for the usual "personal reasons" or to "pursue other opportunities" but for not sharing our values.
>
> Until an organization develops the courage to do this, people will never have full confidence that these soft values are truly real.[20]

Former Transportation Secretary Sam Skinner, a Welch associate and member of the General Electric Board, told me that "Jack Welch's greatest contribution is the example he sets for corporate America in setting high standards of performance by his executives." By creating a thriving meritocracy at GE in place of a stultifying bureaucracy—and by elevating to the top those who not only delivered financial results but who also made respect for and nurturing of people their top priority—Welch did indeed set a leadership example worth emulating.

———◆———

WELCH ON LEADERSHIP: HIRING, FIRING, AND REWARDING EMPLOYEES

- Successful leaders must make very difficult decisions about the people who work for them. The "easy way out" is to treat everyone the same in terms of pay, promotions, and job security—but follow such an approach and your organization will flounder. The top performers will leave or throttle back on effort when they see that no matter how well they do, they will be paid just like everyone else. The average performers will see no incentive to try harder. And the poor performers will likely never leave. They have nowhere to go. They'll just drag you down.

- Telling someone they're not right for your company or organization is the hardest task confronting leaders. But Jack Welch believed it was a form of cruelty to leave such a person in place. It hurts the entire team and it denies that person the push he or she may need to find something more suitable. But firing must be done with humanity.

- Despite possible confrontations and charges of favoritism, giving all employees similar raises is bad for an organization. It is unfair to those who have excelled. The challenge for leaders is to devise a true meritocracy that sets out clear goals for people and gives everyone a chance, but not a guarantee of success. Leaders must ensure that those they reward the best truly are the best, and not just the ones most adept at "impressing the boss."

- "Making the numbers" by itself is not enough to secure pay raises and promotions. Leaders must insist that key players in their organizations also share the values and embrace the culture of that organization. Capable people can at the same time be disruptive and destructive forces, poisoning the work environment and driving other potential star employees out the door.

- Leaders must deftly use the carrots and sticks of pay, promotion, and dismissal to boost productivity and inspire stellar performance. Meritocracy, not bureaucracy, is what you must implement to make your organization excel.

CHAPTER 10

THE LEADER
AS TEACHER

Leadership and learning are indispensable to each other.
—PRESIDENT JOHN F. KENNEDY, NOVEMBER 22, 1963

WHEN JACK WELCH'S overhaul of General Electric
made the transition from the 1980s downsizing and restructuring to the 1990s introduction of openness, sharing, informality, creative conflict, and meritocracy, his focus on people
issues took center stage in his career.

He delivered results to Wall Street—that's all the folks
there needed to hear or know. But inside General Electric and
outside in the business world at large, it was Welch's relentless
search for the far more problematic and less quantifiable values and culture that would attract, retain, train, and motivate
people that established his legacy as a leader worth watching
and following. For all the emphasis Welch-watchers in the
business media—and Welch himself—placed on the solid

earnings reports and sky-high stock values he delivered, those achievements alone do not account for the intense interest in his every utterance and idea.

It was his decision to dive deep into the murky ocean of human behavior and his distinctive ability to communicate his findings from such forays to his own underlings and others that fascinates and excites. He presented the successful leader of today and tomorrow not as a commanding and controlling force, dispassionately maneuvering people and assets around according to some privately hatched and closely guarded master plan—but as a perceptive teacher, motivational coach, and superb communicator.

"The biggest accomplishment I've had is to find great people. An army of them. They are better than most CEOs."[1] GE does indeed boast a stable of quality leaders, but Welch was only partly right in saying he found these leaders. In reality, he was also a major force in creating them.

Welch figured he spent more than half his time as General Electric's chairman on people issues. He wasn't complaining when he reported that; he saw it as just doing his job. "My job is selecting people, evaluating people, giving them self-confidence, building people and spreading ideas," he explained.[2] His oft-repeated line that he didn't run GE, he led GE underscores his people-oriented rather than management-centered conception of leadership. A leader's primary responsibility is to teach, motivate, and inspire, and in so doing, create other leaders. Work-Out, Six Sigma, and the creation of a meritocracy at GE are three pillars of the cultural revolution Jack Welch has engineered at his company. The strategies he launched to teach, mentor, share information, and spread his vision around constitute the fourth pillar.

CROTONVILLE

THE WASHINGTON POST called it "the world's most un-usual and influential business school."[3] It is General Electric's Management Development Institute, known as Crotonville.

Founded in 1956 by then-Chairman Ralph Cordiner, General Electric's Management Development Institute is a 52-acre campus above the Hudson River in a place named Croton-on-Hudson, though everyone calls it Crotonville. It houses some 150 students overnight and is known for its informal, rustic, and quasi-communal atmosphere.

When Jack Welch was growing up, much of his life in Salem, Massachusetts, revolved around the Pit, an excavated gravel area of an abandoned quarry that he and his chums used as a playground. As GE's leader, much of his life was centered in the Pit at Crotonville, a brightly colored lecture hall on the campus where the speaker stands in a well in the center of the room and looks up at the audience all around.

Over the years, Welch taught an average of a class a month here, typically appearing toward the end of students' three-week courses in management and finance. By 1998 he had trained an estimated 15,000 GE managers in some 250 sessions.

"I want to use Crotonville and the Crotonville process to have a cultural revolution in this company," declared Welch, who early in his tenure poured $45 million worth of improvements into the place while he was imposing drastic cutbacks elsewhere.[4]

At the outset, the sessions triggered a cathartic process. Welch reported that he would look up at the class in the early days and see a room full of scowls. "He told workers, many of whom had been given little more power than assembly-line robots under the previous regime, that he wanted their energy," wrote *Investor's Business Daily*. "Seething with 20 years of resentment, they cursed, they lashed out, no holds barred."[5]

A *Business Week* reporter once described a Crotonville session with Jack Welch in the Pit this way: "For nearly four hours he listens, lectures, cajoles, and questions. The managers push right back too."[6]

It's quite a show. "The students see all of Jack here: the management theorist, strategic thinker, business teacher, and corporate icon who made it to the top despite his working class background. No one leaves the room untouched."[7]

While students and teachers—like Welch—are removed from the daily routine of the office and thus freed from the normal duties and conventions of their work, Crotonville's content stays firmly grounded in business reality. "Crotonville has become a vehicle for learning and sharing the best practices that can be found anywhere around the globe," Welch explained. Crotonville combines the thirst for learning of academia within an action environment."[8]

COMMUNICATING, REPEATING . . . AND LISTENING

WELCH CLEARLY SAW his sessions at Crotonville as not only among the most important functions of his job, but the most enjoyable as well. It was a place where he could communicate directly with future generations of GE leaders—and just as important, listen and learn from them. He tried to replicate the Crotonville spirit of interaction and sharing of information and ideas throughout the conduct of company business.

For example, "Meetings around the company that used to consist of self-serving reports and windy speeches became interactive forums for disseminating new ideas and the sharing of experiences," he proclaimed.[9]

Another important ritual of inclusion and communication Welch created was the agenda-setting annual meetings he convened for GE's seniormost 500 executives at various conference center resorts around the country. There managers pitched programs and ideas to the group, with Welch sitting in the front row scribbling copious notes.

At the end of the retreat, it was the CEO who took the floor to deliver an all-encompassing talk in which he reacted to what he heard and shared his own thinking about the year's priorities. By the time the participants returned to their offices, videotapes of Welch's lecture had been delivered company-wide around the world, with translations in several different languages.[10]

It was a "learning company" for everyone at GE, including Welch himself. In the last few years of his tenure, he and other previously Internet- and keyboard-ignorant GE leaders received mentoring from Generation X employees who grew up on the Web. (More on this in Chapter 12.)

Welch also took to heart an observation offered years ago by the savvy former chairman of Citicorp, Walter Wriston— that though CEOs may believe they hold all the cards, they're usually the last to know vital information about how their companies are really operating. Through Crotonville and other listening modes, Welch tried to keep this from happening to him.

President Dwight D. Eisenhower once described leadership as "the art of getting someone else to do something you want done because he wants to do it." Early in his tenure, reports *Business Week,* Welch realized he had to learn Ike's art. "Welch discovered that you can't will things to happen, nor can you simply communicate with a few hundred people at the top and expect change to occur. So he doggedly repeats the same messages over and over again."[11]

According to *Investor's Business Daily,* "It took years [for Welch] to hone complex messages into sound bite principles."[12] As a communications professional, I can state that few communicators in any field have gone as far toward mastering the art of framing arguments and stating principles and ideas in fresh, interesting, and provocative ways as Jack Welch. His clarity, simplicity, and quotability account for the fact that his annual letters to share owners have been so eagerly anticipated and widely digested and disseminated by legions of professionals in business, government, media, and other arenas. The fact that when these interesting and thought-provoking statements are delivered in person, the deliverer is a decidedly unglamorous and unpolished presenter only adds to the credibility and power of the messages themselves.

"Leaders—and you take anyone from Roosevelt to Churchill to Reagan—inspire people with clear visions of how things can be done better," Welch explained. "Some managers, on the other hand, muddle things with pointless complexity and detail. They equate managing with sophistication, with sounding smarter than anyone else. They inspire no one."[13]

For Welch, being simple and clear, articulating a vision and spreading it around, repeating that vision over and over to keep it alive and fresh—and then turning people loose to act on it—was more than just a communications style, it was his management principle: "We weren't managing better. We were managing less and that was better."[14]

LEADERS CREATE LEADERS

"THE BEST LEADERS are really coaches," Jack Welch remarked in his 1997 Letter to Share Owners.[15] Edison Electric Institute President Tom Kuhn has had the opportunity on many occasions to observe Welch in coaching mode. "Jack has tremendous people skills," he told me, "a great instinct for people. That's what stands out to me."

Welch was always proud that his efforts to create leaders at GE resulted in management kudos not only for his company but for other companies that over time have hired away top GE executives. And the methodical, years-long process Welch engineered to train and select his own successor—described in Chapter 14—is testimony to the importance he placed on mentoring, training, and building creative and productive executive talent.

Welch's "most important job has been to train GE's managers of the future," confirmed Canada's *National Post* in a recent analysis of his leadership. "And to that end he has spent more time at GE's in-house university at Crotonville, N.Y., than he has in actually running the company."[16]

He fully expects other executives at the company to follow his lead—for their own success as well as the company's. The most important attribute for the leaders of tomorrow, he insists, will be "to energize an organization, to go out and excite an organization to look outside itself, to engage every person in the place, to get rid of any pomposity, to rid itself of layers—because everyone's going to have the same information."[17]

Through an arduous, ongoing, and constantly evolving series of programs, methodologies, rewards, and penalties, Welch attempted to smash through the bastions of bureaucracy at his organization. He sought to replace a command-and-control culture with a culture of learning and empowerment designed to attract the best talent to his company and unleash a productivity, creativity, and profitability windfall. In his view anyone having trouble making sense of this diffuse corporate conglomerate known as General Electric need look no further than to the company's people to understand what it is really all about:

"Our true 'core competency' is not manufacturing or services, but the global recruiting and nurturing of the world's best people and cultivation in them an insatiable desire to learn, to stretch, and to do things better every day."[18]

WELCH ON LEADERSHIP: LEADERS MUST BE TEACHERS

- Jack Welch spent more than 50 percent of his time as GE's chairman recruiting, training, mentoring, and evaluating company managers and employees—illustrating his conviction that the best leaders are really teachers who instruct and coaches who motivate.

- Today's successful leaders likewise must be prepared to make tremendous investments of time, resources, and energy in attracting, retaining, and inspiring good people. Those who stay hidden behind their office doors or who are too insecure to surround themselves with strong people and share information, thinking, and decisions with them will not succeed.

- Communications is vital to leadership. As we can see with Welch, you do not have to have movie actor looks or top performance skills to be a good communicator—but you must set a clear direction and explain to others in simple terms that both educate and motivate.

- Find the communications devices that work for you. In Jack Welch's case, his sessions at Crotonville, his annual planning meetings, and his yearly letters to shareowners became renowned for their insights and motivational power. As a leader, you should find equivalent approaches to spread your vision around your organization.

CHAPTER 11

LEADERS NEED
A GLOBAL VIEW

The leader has to be practical and a realist, yet must talk
the language of the visionary and the idealist.
—ERIC HOFFER

THE FUTURE OF AMERICA'S economy lies in the global marketplace. It seems like a cliché now, but it was anything but when Jack Welch assumed the helm of General Electric in 1981. In fact, the decade preceding the start of Welch's tenure represented cruel and frustrating years for Americans from the international perspective.

The 1973 Arab oil embargo triggered the nation's first energy crisis, complete with gas lines and energy rationing. When consumers tried to respond by purchasing smaller, more fuel-efficient vehicles, they discovered that it was the Japanese auto industry, not their own, that was ready to meet their needs. The embargo and its wide-ranging impact rudely awakened Americans to the fact that they no longer called all the shots in the post–World War II era and could be held hostage to economic and political forces outside their borders.

Salt was rubbed into this wound in 1975 as Communist forces won a final victory in Southeast Asia with their invasion and takeover of South Vietnam.

Further humiliation overseas came in 1979 when agents of the new radical government of Iran seized and detained American embassy staff in Tehran.

Hobbled by high energy prices, interest rates, taxes, and regulations, the U.S. economy of the late 1970s was devastated by the twin evils of runaway inflation and growing unemployment. Meanwhile, the rival economies of Japan and Germany gained momentum, leading many to wonder whether they would leave America in the dust as a new era of global competitiveness dawned.

The tumultuous 1970s were not the first time that international events and economics had a profound impact on the United States. In fact, international trade has always loomed large in American history. The nation was explored and founded by European countries seeking to develop raw materials and export them to their homelands. During the first half of the 19th century, regional differences over tariffs exacerbated—and some historians say superseded—differences over slavery, leading to the Civil War. As U.S. industrial might and international clout grew in the post–Civil War years, America embarked on a mercantile policy of its own, seeking markets, minerals, raw materials—and colonies—beyond its borders.

When the stock market crashed in 1929, Congress responded with a step many believe transformed a serious recession into the Great Depression—it passed the Smoot-Hawley

Tariff Act of 1930, which contained the highest tariffs and trade restrictions in U.S. history. Following World War II, the United States, now fully engaged and obligated in the global arena, took the lead not only in rebuilding the economies of its enemies and allies but in establishing the legal framework for international commerce, the General Agreement on Tariffs and Trade (GATT). The Bretton Woods Conference in New Hampshire led to the creation of the World Bank, the International Monetary Fund, and the exchange rate system.

Yet after helping to rebuild World War II allies and enemies alike, Americans once again grew complacent. We allowed our own economy to become overtaxed and regulated. Our companies grew fat with bureaucracy in protected domestic markets. And while emerging global competitors concentrated on modernizing their economies and marketing their products worldwide, we were preoccupied with the cold war and were paying most of its high price.

We invited global competitors to our markets while allowing theirs to remain closed and often made poor marketing attempts to capitalize on those that were open. As illustrated by the inroads made here by the Japanese auto industry, U.S. companies and workers frequently learned painful but ultimately productive lessons from these competitors.

But as the 1980s began, Jack Welch and other business leaders had a different vision of America's international potential and economic role in the world. They understood that the new realities of the postwar world—combined with advances in travel and communications and the increasing prowess of U.S. industry, intellectual property, technology, and services—opened huge international opportunities for U.S. companies.

AMERICA—AND GE—
BOOST THEIR GLOBAL PROFILES

TODAY THE PICTURE is vastly different. In the last 30 years of the 20th century, America's international trade exploded. In 2000 U.S. exports to the world totaled $1.068 trillion—triple the level of 1990 and an amount that exceeds the total value of our entire economy just 30 years ago. Vintage American companies like McDonald's and Amway now derive a majority of their revenues and new business outside the borders of the United States.

American business has $1.13 trillion in investments abroad, including $581 billion invested in the European Union, $186 billion in Asia, and $111 billion in Canada. Our corporate presence in other countries has built a strong foundation for economic development. In the special Chinese region of Hong Kong, for example, 10 percent of the workforce is employed by U.S. firms.

U.S. companies are now looking beyond our borders not only for markets and manufacturing but also for services and product development. Now that voice and data can be transmitted easily over the Internet and high-speed fiber optics and satellite communications systems, why not? Computer programmers in India, customer service representatives in the Philippines, and credit card billing processors in Ireland now toil on behalf of U.S. companies and their customers.

Ninety-six percent of the world's consumers live outside the borders of the United States. This simple and stark reality explains GE's commitment to what Jack Welch calls "our oldest initiative"—globalization.

It "began as a search for new markets for our products and services," Welch told shareowners at their annual meeting in April 2001. "That search quickly expanded to include finding the lowest cost, highest quality sources of finished products, components, and raw materials. Today the initiative is so much richer and is focused on talent, searching the world for intellectual capital, driven by the knowledge that the team that fields the best talent from any source wins."[1]

This statement reveals how Welch embraced a concept of globalization far beyond the important but one-dimensional idea of successfully marketing product to overseas customers. His General Electric, in fact, did very well in this regard. Just 20 percent of company revenues were derived from outside the United States in the early 1980s. That increased to 40 percent by the end of his tenure and the company projects it will hit 50 percent before the end of this decade. As the 21st century opens, GE operates in more than 100 countries and employs 313,000 people worldwide.

But Welch took his global view two steps further. First, GE capitalized on a revolution in global logistics that dramatically boosted the speed and efficiency of shipping, transportation, inventory management, data transmission, and financial transactions, as well as of product assembly, sales, and delivery. Companies with the size and smarts to take advantage of these advances—like GE—can build better products more cost-effectively by sourcing materials and components from all over the world. By embracing this view of globalization, Welch and GE were able to wring cost out of the production process and put more speed and quality in— even though a single product in use by consumers may contain parts derived from a dozen or more countries!

A GLOBAL SEARCH FOR TALENT

EVEN MORE RELEVANT for the future of the American economy (and for future leaders in virtually any field) is Welch's insistence on expanding the search for human talent and ideas far beyond the borders of our own country. GE is a company, Welch said, "that searches the world, not just to sell or to source, but to find intellectual capital; the world's best talent and greatest ideas."[2]

Part of Welch's conviction sprang from an understanding of America's changing demographics. American business is finding it increasingly difficult to recruit, train, and retain capable workers at all skill levels. In fact, simply to maintain an average 2.5 percent annual rate of economic growth, our nation will need an additional 300,000 workers per year for the next 15 years—above and beyond anticipated increases in population.

Several factors explain this shortage. America's population is growing older and living longer, but for the most part still leaving the workforce at the same ages (early to mid-60s) that it did in 1950. At the same time, birthrates have declined, so relatively fewer new workers are coming into the workforce. Immigration has been picking up some of this slack and must continue to do so.

And so must reaching out to segments of society that have been traditionally left out or left behind. Like much of corporate America, Welch's GE was criticized in the past for allowing the proverbial "old boys network" to run the show, while failing to foster meaningful professional opportunities for women and minorities. In his review of the year 2000, Welch proudly told shareowners: "Substantial progress was made in

2000 in further diversifying GE's leadership—26 percent of the Company's top 3,900 executives are now women and minorities, and over $30 billion of our 2000 revenues were generated by business operations led by female and minority operating managers."[3]

Regrettably, many of the employees who are available to companies these days have been poorly educated and are ill-equipped for the tasks of the Information Age. The tremendous attention and resources Jack Welch dedicated to training no doubt reflect his passion for excellence—but thanks to a creeping mediocrity in American education, especially at the kindergarten through twelfth grade levels, it was certainly a matter of necessity as well. American business has by default become America's public school system for many workers.

Welch saw GE becoming the "global employer of choice" for the world's talent pool. That doesn't mean he expected all that talent to move to the United States or that it would be managed by American-born executives sent overseas. "American GE business leaders located outside the United States have become fewer and fewer as local leaders, trained in GE operating methods and steeped in our values but with their own unmatchable customer intimacy and market savvy, are replacing them."[4]

Welch also answered critics who claim that globalization has brought with it a degradation of workers' rights and environmental quality. "GE brings only world-class business and work practices and careful, compliant and proactive environmental processes to every one of our global operations," he insisted. "We understand that to be a truly great global company, we must be a great local citizen."[5]

THE CHALLENGES OF GLOBALIZATION

WELCH'S MISSION TO transform GE into a global company was not without challenges, headaches, and missteps. Alongside the undeniable opportunities, going global exponentially multiplies the number of factors, conditions, and risks that can influence and impinge on any company's growth.

Business practices, laws, and cultures vary from region to region. What may be acceptable procedure in one business culture (such as offering payments and other "favors" to secure contracts) is viewed as immoral and illegal in ours. Economic conditions around the globe can vary too. A global company like GE could be having a great earnings year in the United States while taking a financial bath in Asia, Mexico, or Europe. Making wise purchases and choosing good business partners can be challenging enough in the domestic economy. These challenges explode in complexity when, like GE, you are trying to operate profitably in over 100 economies.

Finally there is the role of government. America's global companies must not only conform to the policies, judgments, and whims of Washington, D.C., but those of politicians, bureaucrats, and regulators wherever they operate.

In his quest for globalization, Jack Welch experienced and persevered through all of these potential downsides of going global. Ill-advised contacts on the part of GE with rival diamond producer DeBeers of South Africa led to price-fixing allegations and a celebrated trial (during which the charges were dismissed). Welch's acquisition of France's CGR, one of Europe's biggest makers of X-ray machines, was later panned by critics as a costly drain.

Economic turmoil in key international markets tested GE's nerve as well, but also underscored Welch's belief in a long-term vision that resists overreaction to short-term events. With a significant 9 percent of GE revenues dependent on Asia when it hit, the 1997 Asian financial crisis provided such a lesson and a test.

"We, like everyone else, had not foreseen these difficulties," Welch conceded, "but we quickly viewed Asia as similar in many respects to the Europe of the early 1990s—in need of various structural remedies but rich in opportunity. In the case of Europe—and in the case of Mexico in the mid-90s—we moved decisively and were rewarded with significant and rapid growth."[6]

As of 2001, much of Asia has largely recovered from the crisis—though Japan is still floundering. But in Welch's view, giving up on a market with the size and potential of Japan would be like giving up on Mexico and Europe in those earlier years. For that matter, he emphasized, it would be akin to giving up on the United States itself!

"We've been down this path before," he pointed out. "In the early 1980s, we experienced a United States mired in recession, hand wringing from the pundits, and dirges being sung over American manufacturing. We didn't buy this dismal scenario; instead we invested in both a widespread restructuring and in new businesses. We emerged into the recovery a much more productive and competitive company."[7]

As he had done with Europe, Mexico, and the United States, Welch kept his eye on the longer-term horizon as Asia slid precipitously toward depression. "The path to greatness in Asia is irreversible," he proclaimed, "and GE will be there."[8]

Yet it wasn't until his closing months at the helm of GE that Jack Welch experienced his most bitter taste of the downside of globalization—as European Union bureaucrats and officials wrecked GE's $45 billion merger with Honeywell, claiming that the new company—without major divestitures—would run afoul of E.U. antitrust laws.

It was proof positive that in a global environment, pleasing your own government is not enough. Indeed, many observers have suggested that given the current state of competitiveness and rancor between the United States and Europe, not to mention the decidedly left-of-center complexion of the E.U. government, Welch should have anticipated such problems. After all, the E.U. had already tried to scuttle the merger of Boeing and McDonnell Douglas and actually succeeded in the case of MCI WorldCom and Sprint.

Fair or unfair, operating in a new global environment requires intimate knowledge not only of markets, consumer tastes, and business cultures but also of governments.

None of these trials shook Jack Welch from his "oldest initiative." Ultimately the global view Welch insists great companies and leaders must have is as much an attitude and an intellectual posture as it is a marketing, procurement, or employment strategy. It is an attitude of openness to new ideas, diverse people, and different cultures regardless of their origins. It is an intellectual demeanor of immense curiosity that soaks up the best practices, approaches, styles, and tastes from all over the world. It rejects the provincial, the protectionist, the isolationist and xenophobic sentiments that close minds and breed complacency, arrogance, and ignorance. Welch's own experience and record teaches aspiring leaders in all fields the essentiality of this broader global view.

It is a view that still allows ample room for patriotism. Even as he extended his company's reach around the world, Welch still marveled at what distinguishes his country from the others: "The U.S. system has the most free enterprise in the world, with Britain next," he once told *Fortune* magazine. After that, it falls off dramatically. "What our system has is freedom. It allows people like me to become chairman of GE in one generation, it allows the talented young engineers in our company to move up fast."[9]

The future of America's economy lies in the global marketplace. Those who understand that will be its future leaders.

WELCH ON LEADERSHIP: LEADERS NEED A GLOBAL VISION

- Beginning in the early 1980s, Jack Welch was at the forefront of a movement to reassert the U.S. role in the international economic arena and boost flagging U.S. competitiveness. During his tenure he more than doubled the portion of GE revenues that come from overseas operation.

- In the 21st century successful leaders will be those who, like Welch, have a global vision. For companies, this vision includes taking advantage of new market opportunities for products and services among the 96 percent of the world's population that resides outside the United States. Thanks to technology and improved shipping and logistics, even smaller companies can seize such opportunities.

- A global vision also means sourcing from around the world—products, information, capital, and people. Internet communications along with efficient shipping and travel have turned the globe into a massive storefront from which companies and organization can choose the best materials and attract the most lucrative financing and creative people.

- In the broadest sense, leaders with a global vision are those whose minds are open to new ideas, different approaches, and diverse people. With the U.S. population becoming increasingly diverse—and with technology enabling the linkages of research institutions, laboratories, and universities around the globe—successful leaders will be those who reject the provincial in favor of the worldly.

- At the same time, if globalization has created a host of new opportunities for today's leaders, it has also created legions of new competitors. Keeping up with the global competition is critical not only to play on their turf but to keep them from grabbing yours!

CHAPTER 12

CREATING "E-JACK": JACK WELCH JOINS THE INTERNET REVOLUTION

The quality of a leader is reflected in the standards they set for themselves.
—RAY KROC

IN THE YEAR 2000, it was the 122-year-old General Electric company that was declared the "e-business of the year" by both *InternetWeek* and *WORTH* magazines. Not Amazon, not Dell Computer, not Microsoft, but that old lion of American business—GE.

Jack Welch explained why his company deserved such an honor in his last report to shareholders as General Electric CEO, delivered in April 2001. "Moving our traditional customers to the Web for much more efficient transactions has been very successful," he announced. "And in 2000, we sold $8 billion in goods and services online, a number that'll grow to $20 billion this year, making this . . . institution one of the biggest, if not the biggest, e-Business company in the world."[1]

It was a remarkable turn of events for a company whose leader two years earlier was a self-described Internet "Neanderthal" who couldn't type—a leader who had recently stood before hundreds of CEOs at a conference and all but bragged about not having or needing a computer in his office.

By his own admission, Jack Welch came very late to the Internet revolution. Before he left GE he was one of its chief evangelists and GE one of its most successful practitioners. And who said you can't teach old dogs new tricks?

Not that Welch ever bought into all the vapory New Age rhetoric about the so-called New Economy. "The Internet revolution is the biggest revolution in business history since the industrial revolution," he explained to the *Economic Times* shortly after his 2001 report to shareowners. "But it's only a technology, its not a New Economy. . . . Centuries ago people sold something and people bought something. But they did it in a cart and a horse, in a farm or in a square.

"What's happening in this New Economy? People are buying, people are selling. But they're doing it now with a different technology."[2]

JANE WELCH'S DISCOVERY

WHAT TRIGGERED Welch's late conversion to the possibilities of the Internet? His interest was piqued in mid to late 1998 as he observed what was going on around him in the hallways and offices of GE—employees and colleagues going online for information and Christmas shopping. Then, shortly after Christmas that year, Welch was hooked by his wife, Jane, with a most irresistible lure. She told him that any given time he could log on to sites and see all the good—and nasty—things investors and other surfers were saying about him in chat rooms.

"I went to Mexico to celebrate my 10th anniversary with my wife," he related to *Newsweek* and in other interviews. "She started showing me Yahoo investor sites, where people were talking about GE stock. 'Jack's a jerk, Jack's great, Jack should do this.' My God it was fascinating. So I started sneaking in from the pool during the rest of the vacation to look at it."[3]

Returning from vacation, Welch set out to conquer a barrier that stood in the way of his newfound desire to be a Net surfer—he couldn't type! So with the help of an interactive CD-ROM course, he spent several weekends teaching himself how to pound the keyboard.

It wasn't long before Welch began to "connect the dots" between his own experiences as a freshly minted Net enthusiast and the impact this technology could have on General Electric's businesses and culture. He wound up singing the praises of Internet technology for a company like GE with the fervor of a Sunday preacher, while always cautioning his flock that such technology is a means to an end not an end in itself.

WELCH ON THE "DOT-COMS"

FOR THIS REASON, Welch never placed much stock in firms whose entire business plans were based on e-commerce and appeared thoroughly unsurprised as the dot-com bubble burst in late 2000. In his November 2000 interview on *60 Minutes*, Welch told a group of his managers, "Don't let somebody show up with a dot-com. It's nothing. It's meaningless."

But in other interviews he was more reflective on the contribution these companies, whether they live or die, have made to American business. "I'm not pooh-poohing the dot-coms," Welch told one interviewer. "They grabbed the technology and gave us all a light in the right direction. . . . But it turns out what they did—digitizing, creating Web sites—was the easiest part of the whole process. Building plants, having fulfillment, creating processes—that's the hard part. Digitalization isn't brain surgery."[4]

Though he recognized the role that start-ups and entrepreneurs have played in ushering in the Internet Age, Welch saw most of the business bounty accruing to bigger, more established companies. One immediate manifestation of the collapse of many dot-coms and the evaporation of investor capital has been a stanching of the flow of executive and engineering talent from companies like GE to technology companies. Never missing a beat in his drive to draw the best from the world's talent pool, Welch was quick to offer a sales pitch in the wake of the dot-com wreckage: "If you're interested in learning about digitalization, GE is the place to be," he said.

While acknowledging that a few dot-com originals will survive, Welch remained persuaded that the "Internet belongs to the big and the old." "Every advantage accrues to the big and the old. Brand is important. Fulfillment is important, loyalty is important to the Net."[5]

A plausible premise, to be sure, but how difficult was it to take a company like GE into the Internet Age?

Welch confesses that the company started with a limited vision that led it down some unproductive paths. "We started out with some things that were not the greatest ideas," he explained to *Newsweek*. "We originally thought we had to set up entrepreneurs in separate buildings, doing wild Web things away from the main company. But they were isolated, out of the mainstream, so we brought them back."[6]

Welch also lashes himself for focusing too much on the e-commerce staples of buying and selling online, while almost missing the potential of the Internet to save money and improve quality in the actual process of making product and developing services. "I didn't realize until later that it's what I call the make side, not just the buy or sell sides, that presents the biggest opportunity for big business."[7]

THE INTERNET AND WELCH'S LEADERSHIP VALUES

TODAY THAT SEEMS like a logical, almost obvious, conclusion for a man who resolutely believes that the Internet is ultimately a tool—albeit a very, very powerful tool—whose greatest promise is that it can be put to work in pursuit of older and more timeless Welch values.

Indeed when you run down a list of the most important values Welch attempted to instill at GE from the earliest days of his leadership, it is striking how many can be advanced by Internet technology. It's a synergy that surely explains the CEO's self-described "gonzo" enthusiasm for digitalization.

He went on a two-decades-long quest to wring waste, inefficiency, and excess cost out of GE so as to maximize earnings. Welch was very precise on how the Internet will aid this cause: "By digitalizing our processes from customer service to travel and living, we'll take over a billion dollars of cost out of our operations this year [2001] alone."[8] That's real money! So is the 10 cents per share of additional earnings Welch figures his technology initiatives will add to the bottom line.

He wanted to lead a company that moves quickly to embrace new products, improve old ones, and meet customer needs. Speed counts. Welch painted this picture of how the Web can accelerate this goal: "What we are rapidly moving toward is the day when 'Dr. Jones' in radiology can go to her home page in the morning and find a comparison of the number, and clarity, of scans her CT machines performed in the last day, or week, to more than 10,000 other machines around the world. She will then be able to click and order software solutions that will bring her performance up to world-class levels. And the performance of her machines might have been improved, online, the previous night, by a GE engineer in Milwaukee, Tokyo, Paris or Bangalore."[9]

He wanted GE to be a truly global company working on a 24/7 basis all over the world. The Internet has given a tremendous boost to companies and organizations with interests around the world, with easier communication alone worth the price of admission. Welch spoke excitedly of a global community of engineers and product and software designers working in concert yet in disparate locations to solve problems, upgrade designs, and meet customer needs. In particular, information technology empowered GE to tap into distant but invaluable centers of knowledge and intellectual capital. "Our use of the intellect [in India] has far outpaced my wildest dreams," he remarked on a recent visit to that country. "Software development, design centers, building a new corporate laboratory in Bangalore. . . . We do more sourcing of brains from India than any other country outside of the U.S."[10] The Internet has made it possible.

He wanted to shut down stifling bureaucracy and create in GE that boundaryless organization. Perhaps most emotionally satisfying of the benefits ascribed to the Internet by Welch was its potential for negative impact on the reviled corporate bureaucracy and for positive impact on efforts to create a company without boundaries in which employees from shop floor to executive suite can participate. The Internet is the "ultimate boundary buster—the final nail in the coffin for bureaucracy at GE," Welch proclaimed, perhaps too optimistically.[11] But the direction he set forth is clear—at GE digitalization was as much about changing internal processes and culture as about making sales and procuring components and supplies.

He wanted to lead a company whose stock in trade is turning managers into leaders. Welch poured enormous amounts of personal time and company resources into training and mentoring. The arrival of the Internet Age at GE has afforded yet another opportunity to highlight this priority, but this time with a twist—the young teaching the old. When it came to inculcating the GE culture and workforce with Internet prowess, Welch realized he needed to tap into the "wildness of youth." A mentoring program was created for nearly 1,000 GE managers who received Internet training from younger members of the staff. Welch's own mentors included the young employee who now runs the company's Web site. And in a lighthearted vein, the CEO also credited his younger-generation wife: "She was all over this computer stuff. Having a second wife 17 years younger than you can get you in the game faster. I wouldn't advise that technique for everyone, but it worked for me."[12]

He strove for a culture of informality where the people within the organization could interact and speak their minds, free of the stuffy and stultifying rituals and protocols of corporate America. Jack Welch maintained more than his share of the trappings of the modern corporate scion—the plane, the helicopter, the limousines, and the handlers. But with new technology companies came a new breed of business executive that emphasized precisely the kind of informality in attire, in management, in communications with employees, and in personal style that Jack Welch championed for years. Of course the rituals and stylistics of the new CEOs are as easily stereotyped and lampooned as the old. (How many times in photos, on TV, or in in-person presentations have you seen an executive attired in open shirt and khakis, perched in a director's chair, a wireless microphone in the lapel and an ever-present bottle of designer water at one side?) Still, as can be seen by his rapport with Sun Microsystems's Scott McNealy, who was recently named to GE's Board of Directors, the retirement-aged Welch is clearly at home with brash and irreverent executives of the Internet era.

All along, the rationale behind Welch's business plan was to build an enterprise with the body of a big company and the soul of a small one. Clearly, the challenges and opportunities presented by the Internet posed a major test for Welch's belief that these two qualities could in fact be combined in a single entity. Could a company as massive as General Electric act with the nimbleness and speed usually attributed to small companies and embrace the potential of digitalization—not just in rhetoric or in a few limited applications, but throughout its global architecture and culture?

Welch thinks GE has made the grade, despite his belief that when it comes to e-business the American economy on the whole is still in the "first inning." As for his company: "Against our competitive playing field, we're ahead of the game. Against an absolute standard, we're behind the game."[13]

Leading technology executives are generally more charitable. "I would say that GE very clearly is outrunning the other traditional hikers in its businesses," says Sun Microsystems's McNealy.[14]

John Chambers, president and CEO of Cisco Systems, concurs—and marvels at Welch's ability to grasp an idea and quickly spread it throughout a huge organization. "Eighteen months ago, Welch didn't have the Internet on his top 10 agenda," Chambers told a London newspaper in November 2000. "The company was headed one way, and he said, 'Let's turn.' And they turned on a dime. GE went from the edge of the pool to break-neck speed, faster than any other major company out of the Industrial Revolution has ever done it. I mean, we're good, but they're better."[15]

On a personal level, the 65-year-old Welch still maintains his fondness for the communications tools of an earlier era. He credits e-mail with enabling him to reach down into his organization—beyond those who report directly to him. But e-mail never stopped the flow of handwritten notes—faxed and then mailed—for which Welch was famous. "I don't find it as easy to communicate as passionately by e-mail," he told *Fortune* magazine in a May 2000 joint interview with

McNealy. "Somehow the thickness of the pen makes me feel better; it makes it feel more meaningful to me."

Hearing this, the 40-something high-tech executive McNealy volunteered: "If you sent me a written note, I'd never get it."[16]

Jack Welch's relatively late embrace of the Internet—followed by his productive effort to turn GE "on a dime" to become a leader in a wide range of Internet applications and capabilities—offers another key component of the Welch formula for successful leadership:

You don't have to invent the change or be the first to forecast it to capitalize on it. You can even come a little late to the party. But then you must embrace it, put your own unique stamp on it, and communicate the reasons for its importance to your entire team so that they in turn will move your organization. No matter what your age or station in life or in work, always keep your mind open to new approaches and opportunities. Be willing to learn from the old and the young.

You don't have to always make the waves, but a leader figures out how to ride their crests.

WELCH ON LEADERSHIP:
EMBRACING THE INTERNET

- Jack Welch came late to the Internet party. His experience illustrates both the danger of resisting change and the capacity of a great leader to embrace it.

- Internet technology is an incredible tool, but in the end it is just a tool. Leaders must harness it and turn it to their advantage in their organizations, but not see it as an end in itself.

- Debates about the New Economy versus the Old Economy miss the point about the role of technology in our lives. Business has always been and will always remain someone selling something and someone buying something—for companies, the Internet can improve the process but will not change the fundamental equation.

- The Internet can be very useful for those leaders striving to create a boundaryless, informal, and flat organization where everyone's ideas and involvement are welcomed. For those clinging to the old "command and control" and information-hoarding styles of management, the Internet will make their task difficult if not impossible.

- As Welch's and GE's experience with the Internet shows, it's never too late to embrace a new approach, technology, or business methodology. The best leaders will always be open to new ways of doing things, but like Welch, will view such innovations practically.

- Jack Welch wanted to create a "learning company" at GE but never forgot that he would have to continually learn as well. When it came to the Internet and GE, the bosses became the students and the underlings became the teachers. Only secure and self-confident leaders allow such an environment!

CHAPTER 13

THE COURAGE
TO CHANGE

———————

A real leader faces the music, even when he doesn't like the tune.
—ANONYMOUS

READINESS, EVEN EAGERNESS, to embrace change
has been a Jack Welch passion from his first days as leader of
General Electric, and it surely ranks among the top qualities
he looks for and recommends in other leaders. Don't just tolerate change, relish it, love it!

"We've long believed that when the rate of change inside
an institution becomes slower than the rate of change outside,
the end is in sight. The only question is when," Welch wrote
in his last letter to shareowners as CEO. "Learning to love
change is an unnatural act in any century-old institution, but
today we have a Company that does just that: sees change always as a source of excitement, always as opportunity, rather
than as threat or crisis."[1]

With his late but fervent embrace of the Internet, his ninth-inning blockbuster attempt to acquire Honeywell, and with his evolution from the hard-nosed corporate cost-cutter to the seemingly more benign corporate coach and empowerer, the GE leader surely lived up to his rhetoric. But in these cases and others, Welch could point to changing circumstances, an altered business or technology environment, or new opportunities as being the catalysts for change. In these instances it was relatively easy for Welch to embrace the change, master it, and demonstrate how it would benefit his company and in fact amplify GE's core values and economic strength.

But what happens when a prominent leader is asked to question, challenge, or even discard one of the central premises of a whole leadership approach? A real leader has the courage or capacity to reconsider premises—and the humility and self-confidence to announce that a long-promoted remedy, something widely emulated and celebrated by others, is finally being put out to pasture.

Jack Welch confronted precisely this dilemma late in his career when the viability of one of his most famous and widely copied management prescriptions was called into question: Be number one or number two in every business you're in—or get out.

In the 1980s, as Welch struggled to restructure and refocus the company for a new era of rapid globalization and cutthroat competition he saw coming, the "number one–number two" tenet became the mantra of GE. First mentioned in his maiden speech to analysts in 1981, by 1985 it was a familiar Welch refrain. He explained its purpose and importance in the strongest of terms:

"Where we are not number one or number two, and don't have or can't see a route to a technological edge, we've got to ask ourselves Peter Drucker's very tough question," Welch insisted. "'If you weren't already in the business, would you be in it today?'"[2]

If the answer is no, he continued, the company's response must be to fix, sell, or close that business.

"The managements and companies in the '80s that don't do this, that hang onto losers for whatever reason—tradition, sentiment, their own management weakness—won't be around in 1990," he forecast early in his tenure. "We believe this central idea—being number one or number two—more than an objective—a requirement—will give us a set of businesses which will be unique in the business world equation at the end of the decade."

In other statements, Welch became even more adamant. "Don't play with businesses that can't win," he decreed. "Businesses that are number 3, number 5 in their market— Christ couldn't fix those businesses. They're going to lose anyway."[3]

PLAYING GAMES YOU CAN WIN

SOME INTERPRETED Welch's number one–number two edict as a manifestation of either a compulsion to win and best the competition at any cost, or the flip side, an aversion to tough competition. Being able to say he and his company were number one or number two was more important, they suggested, than assembling the best mix of profitable businesses. (A company doing no better than third in markets of sufficient size could still be a successful and hugely profitable enterprise, could it not?) Stacking the deck by refusing to compete unless victory was assured evidenced an excessive vanity and even insecurity.

In fact, Welch's approach to competition and achievement in both business and life has always been more creative and strategic. The fight, if you will, was never an end in itself. "Some people say I'm afraid to compete. I think one of the jobs of a businessperson is to get away from the slugfests and into niches where you can prevail," he explained. "The fundamental goal is to get rid of weakness, to find a sheltered womb where no one can hurt you.

"There's no virtue in looking for a fight. If you're in a fight, your job is to win. But if you can't win, you've got to find a way out."[4]

Other choices Welch made in life, outside business, reflect a similar philosophy. As a youth and young man his sport of choice evolved from baseball to hockey to golf. Understanding the upper limits of his potential and the competition he would be up against—no matter how hard he worked— played a key role in his changing tastes. "My hockey was good in high school, but I never got any better." In the eighth and ninth grades Welch also remembers being "the best pitcher in Salem. I was pitching against seniors, but then by the time I was a senior I was on the bench, because I never got any faster. . . . Same thing in college. In high school I was on the all-star hockey team. In college? I couldn't skate fast enough. I topped out in sports so early, except for golf."[5]

Welch credits his wife, Jane, with vastly improving his golf game, albeit in a roundabout way. She couldn't play and asked her husband to teach her. Once again, the value and rewards that come from coaching and mentoring—which Welch made such a critical part of the GE culture—proved themselves to the CEO: "By teaching her, I focused on golf in a way that I'd never done. And I've gone to a whole new level."[6]

A young Jack Welch tested his "smart competition" theory when choosing colleges as well. "If I had gone to the Massachusetts Institute of Technology I would have been down at the bottom of the pile and never got my head out. By going to a small state school [the University of Massachusetts] I was fortunate enough to get a lot of self-confidence," he relates. "I had some kids in my high school who did better than I did, so instead of going to UMass, they went to MIT. And they ended up in the middle of the pack among some of the brightest kids in the country. . . . I mean I was a golden boy in chemical engineering at UMass."[7]

Choosing his undergraduate studies strategically paid off because his good grades produced fellowships and several options for graduate school. Welch employed the same factors in this decision as well. "I went to the University of Illinois, which had a great reputation in engineering, and I had a lot of places to go because I was in the top of the class at a school that wasn't MIT, so it was easier to shine in this pond."[8]

Welch's competitive ethos, embodied in the number one–number two dictum, has been compared to locker room bravado, but these episodes illustrate a more complex and commonsensical approach.

At GE, Welch's early task was to convince a proud institution with a great history and hidebound traditions that it had to move in bold new directions in a dramatically changing business environment. Articulating and instilling the number one–number two philosophy throughout the organization gave it a rationale and a rallying cry as Welch's dramatic restructuring was carried out. It helped make sense of the change. It brought order to the disorder. It helped explain tough decisions about buying and selling businesses—and letting people go. Most important, it cried out reasonableness. It drew boundaries of conduct and purpose around the businesspeople under Welch's purview in the cutthroat competitive environment of the 1980s. These boundaries in effect said: When competing in business, don't be bloodthirsty or timid. Be practical and be smart.

As recently as the letter to shareowners he penned in 1996 (reviewing 1995), Welch was singing the praises of one of his most frequently cited business provisos. "The foundation for our future was to be involved in only those businesses that were, or could become, either number one or number two in their global markets," he wrote. "The rest were to be fixed, sold or closed. We made this decision based on our observation that when a number one market-share business entered a down cycle, and 'sneezed,' number four or number five often caught galloping pneumonia."[9]

Other companies nationally and internationally adopted similar strategies. In a special report on Welch's theory, *USA Today* cites Johnson & Johnson as an example of another company that acquired dozens of companies "so that 75 percent of its sales are from products or businesses that are No. 1 or No. 2."[10] Earthgrains has achieved a first or second ranking in 24 of its 27 markets, thanks to the baker's own GE-style strategy. Overseas the approach has been pursued by firms ranging from Vodaphone of Great Britain to Boral, the Australian construction materials concern.

ONE-TWO LOSES ITS LUSTER

FLASH-FORWARD TO Jack Welch's final letter to shareowners as General Electric's CEO, released in February 2001. Amid the slew of statistics documenting another record-breaking year for GE performance, embedded in the seven pages of pithy Welchisms on subjects ranging from technology to bureaucracy to the value of informality came this bombshell:

> One of GE's long-standing management tenets has been the belief that businesses must be, or become, number one or number two in their marketplaces. We managed by that tenet for years, and enjoyed the business success that came, over time, from implementing it. But, once again, insidious bureaucracy crept into the definition of number one or number two and began to lead management teams to define their markets more and more narrowly to assure that their business would fit the one-or-two share definition.[11]

In sum, Welch discovered that what had once been a sharp-edged, motivating rallying cry had over time metamorphosed into a comfortable cocoon of security for timid managers and business developers. The tenet was used by some as an excuse to dismiss forward-looking ideas, imaginative thinking, and new opportunities. Instead of inspiring boldness, it began to justify timidity.

Welch's public explanation for the shift in strategy—bureaucrats who were supposedly snuffed out a long time ago at GE had spoiled a good idea—is somewhat disappointing. But how he came to this conclusion and the fact that he made the change testifies to the culture of freewheeling "boundarylessness" he worked so hard to instill.

"It took a mid-level Company management training class reporting out to us in the spring of 1995 to point out, without shyness or sugar-coating, that our cherished management idea had been taken to nonsensical levels," he explained. "They told us we were missing opportunities, and limiting our growth horizons by shrinking our definition of 'the market' in order to satisfy the requirement to be number one or number two.

"This fresh view shocked us, and we shocked the system."[12] GE began defining markets in such a way that reduced the shares of many GE businesses to 10 percent or less—thereby emphasizing untapped potential rather than the complacency that can come with knowing or believing that you already dominate those markets.

Welch's strategic shift was greeted as the business world's equivalent of "Nixon going to China." As more details of the change emerged, the story became even more intriguing.

To start, the changeover was triggered all the way back in 1995—yet Welch didn't announce it until the release of his final CEO letter to shareowners in February 2001. The company has since explained that it kept the new policy under wraps for competitive reasons. Putting his company first always (and certainly above his role as a business guru, which has for the most part been thrust upon him by others), Welch apparently felt no compunction about hiding his own mid-course correction from other companies still following his old dictum.

Furthermore, the process by which GE leaders received what Welch calls their "punch in the nose" featured not only middle-level company managers but outsiders as well. In 1995 these managers found themselves in a brainstorming session at the historic site of the battle of Gettysburg with officers of the U.S. Army War College. During a wide-ranging discussion on how the lessons of war could be applied to business, and vice versa, a colonel from the War College wondered out loud whether GE's number one–number two strategy was causing the company to miss opportunities.

According to an account in *USA Today,* the remark was greeted with an audible gasp by many of the GE managers present that day. But after the initial shock passed, a penetrating discussion ensued—and its conclusions later made their way up the ladder to Welch.

The GE leader portrayed the shift as more of a relaxation of a policy, not abandonment. Even so he called the adjustment "a better idea" and "a major factor in our acceleration to double-digit revenue growth rates in the latter half of the '90s."[13]

What does this episode reveal about Welch's leadership approach and the lessons it offers for aspiring leaders? Here you have a man who is the nation's most admired CEO. He is lionized and widely imitated by his peers. He is brash and headstrong and full of self-confidence, with an enviable business track record that is hard to match. And at age 65 he is near the end of his corporate career and presumably quite set in his ways. He has been told many times by many people how great he is.

It would be perfectly understandable to see him cling un-shakably to one of the core ideas that made him successful and famous.

But the best leaders don't do that. They stay open to new ideas. They encourage fresh thinking and don't care where in-side or outside the organization it comes from. They check and recheck their fondest and most familiar premises. Where appropriate they have the courage to change.

But the challenge goes beyond such fortitude. Over 150 years ago Ralph Waldo Emerson wrote, "Consistency is the hobgoblin of little minds." But many others have since ob-served that far from being an affliction of a little mind, being consistent can also mean you are standing on principle and refusing to act like a human weather vane, shifting direction every time the wind of popular opinion change.

In leadership there can be a fine line between the kind of change that reflects new conditions and fresh thinking—and the kind of change that displays lack of a moral compass and deficient commitment to principle. Ultimately the true leader maintains not only great courage but good judgment too. One needs both to tell the difference.

WELCH ON LEADERSHIP: THE COURAGE TO CHANGE

- Great leaders embrace change and are excited by the opportunities change creates. They also create compelling visions and spread them throughout their organizations. These visions help people make sense of their jobs, the mission of their organization, and the reasoning behind executive decisions.

- Yet sometimes changing conditions force a leader's initial vision to change as well. In Welch's case, his idea of maintaining only those businesses that were or could be number one or number two in their fields worked for many years. But changes in the global economy and within GE later rendered it less effective and even harmful. The key test for Welch was whether he could see that and would be willing to jettison or seriously alter one of his most cherished and celebrated management principles. He was able to do that—would you be able to do the same?

- In today's ever-changing world, great ideas have a limited shelf life. What works today may not work tomorrow. A key challenge for leaders in any field is to know when to embrace and when to discard approaches—and to maintain this willingness to change no matter how long they've been in charge, no matter where the advice to change comes from, and no matter how fond they are of the "good old days" when a particular idea built their organization and their reputation.

CHAPTER 14

SUCCESSION:
A LEADER'S FINAL TEST

The final test of a leader is that he leaves behind him in other men
the conviction and the will to carry on.
—WALTER LIPPMANN

It was the toughest decision I ever made in my life.
—JACK WELCH ON CHOOSING A SUCCESSOR

THE SUSPENSE ENDED on November 27, 2000. After a six-year process and an 18-month horse race with three "gold medal" finalists, Jack Welch introduced 44-year-old Jeffrey R. Immelt as General Electric's next chairman and CEO.

The secret was closely guarded and handled with typical Jack Welch panache. Once Welch and his board finalized the decision, the CEO summoned Immelt back from a South Carolina vacation and then hopped on board a company jet to personally tell two other contenders that they had not been selected. At the announcement press conference just days later, Welch underscored the careful planning and deliberation that had gone into his selection, noting proudly that "six years ago we decided to announce this in December 2000." He had beaten a timetable devised long ago by two weeks![1]

Just the same, with his announcement, Welch started down the pockmarked path that has tripped up many leaders in the past and will surely do so in the future—planning and preparing for the time when they must turn the reins of leadership over to successors.

For GE, the transition process is doubly daunting. The company has had less than a dozen leaders after more than a century in business. Some of these forebears have been enshrined by historians as giants in American industry. To top it off, the outgoing occupant of the corner office is someone routinely described as an American icon—*Fortune* magazine's "Manager of the Century" no less—whose every prescription and prognostication is eagerly lapped up by avid admirers.

The company's performance has been solid and often stellar throughout Welch's 20-year reign, even during the several economic downturns that checkered the period. Before Welch could leave the CEO's chair, speculation was already spreading that once his sheer force of will was no longer standing in the way, the laws of gravity would finally take over and disparate GE businesses—from broadcasting to financial services—would soon come flying apart.

Moreover, the recent track record of other successions in corporate America has been spotty at best. Analysts are quick to cite Gillette, Xerox, and Procter & Gamble as just three examples of rocky transitions from the old guard to the new.

SUCCESSION OFTEN NEGLECTED

IN FACT, GIVEN ALL that is at stake in succession—the incumbent leader, the freshly minted one, their organization's legacy, and all those with a vested interest in it—it is remarkable how little attention is paid to the process, how frequently it is simply turned over to outsiders, and how often it is botched. That goes for politics, nonprofit organizations, small businesses, and families as well as for corporate America.

Some very human factors explain much of this condition.

After all, who really wants to think about that inevitable time when we're no longer around? Paving the way for a successor reminds us that we're mortal, that power is fleeting, and that institutions—and life—will go on without us. (No doubt this feeling helps explain why a majority of Americans have never prepared a will.)

Insecure leaders sometimes fail to equip would-be successors with the training and knowledge they need to take over to heighten their own sense of indispensability. Or they choose weak underlings who pose no threat, thereby making themselves look smart by comparison. Being surrounded by strong and creative people, including one or more potential replacements, insecure bosses figure, only confirms their own replaceability.

In some circumstances it is possible that those in line for possible promotion to the top job don't enjoy the confidence of the incumbent. The top dog doesn't want to keep them in the loop or groom them, hoping instead they'll just go somewhere else. Perhaps the number two candidate was chosen by others or selected for reasons other than personal ability.

More reasonable explanations for a lack of attention to or involvement in succession planning on the part of incumbents is the theory that they should stay out of the process. That it's an act of arrogance and egotism to do otherwise. Fairness, the need to avoid mistakes born of excessive loyalty to long-time underlings, and the desire to infuse the organization with fresh leadership draw many leaders to the conclusion they should leave succession to others. Others fear that triggering a horse race among several top deputies will create office politics and infighting and undercut the organization's performance. And often the need to choose from several highly talented underlings who are also personal friends the leader doesn't want to disappoint—as Jack Welch had to do—is simply too emotionally difficult a decision to make. Why not leave it others?

The American vice presidency offers some interesting perspectives on the issue of executive succession. In the early years of the republic, the runners up for the top prize ended up in the number-two slot. The president had no reason to trust his vice president. There was little or no common agenda. Thus there was no motivation to keep the vice president in the loop or groom him to take over.

As the years went on, the political parties grew in strength. Regional differences became more prominent. Vice presidential nominees were then chosen to reward party loyalty or provide regional balance for the upcoming election campaign. In the second half of the 20th century, a host of other criteria came into play. Sometimes vanquished primary opponents were chosen to foster party unity—as with John F. Kennedy's choice of Lyndon Johnson in 1960 and Ronald Reagan's choice of George Bush in 1980. Others were chosen in large part to make a symbolic point to important constituencies, such as Walter Mondale's selection of Geraldine Ferraro in 1984.

None of these factors led to the creation of a strong vice presidency whose occupants work in close concert with the president and are fully prepared and qualified to take over if necessary—just the opposite. Even the arrival of modern warfare, split-second communications, and nuclear weapons failed to change the basic approach as vice presidents such as Harry Truman, Lyndon Johnson, and Spiro Agnew found themselves in the dark and even ostracized by the Roosevelt, Kennedy, and Nixon presidential staffs.

No wonder an earlier Roosevelt vice president, John Nance Garner, disparagingly described his job as not worth a bucket of warm . . . er . . . spit!

Fortunately for the nation, in recent times our would-be White House occupants have taken a more serious, corporate-style approach to the critical number-two position. The close teamwork and trust between Jimmy Carter and Walter Mondale significantly altered the relationship between the two offices.

Some of their successors raised the bar further. Breaking with tradition, Bill Clinton chose Al Gore for his running mate, not because Gore was different but because he was similar. Both men were similar in age, hailed from the same region, and shared a common ideology. Gore was a trusted adviser, handled important projects, and was anointed early on by the president and his staff as Clinton's preferred successor. George W. Bush was so intent on making qualifications paramount that he chose in Dick Cheney a man from a small state (Wyoming) who had both executive and Washington experience but whose own designs on the presidency are nonexistent.

The world of politics may have learned a few lessons from the world of business—but when it comes to succession business still has a long way to go. Many small, family-owned enterprises never make it past a single generation because of the owners' lack of attention to succession and estate planning. Many larger organizations have drawn up contingency plans for emergencies. They know who will step in should the boss's corporate jet go down, but they have spent little time preparing for much less remote probabilities—the basically inevitable day when the baton will be passed.

CREATE A TALENT POOL

ULTIMATELY THE DEPTH of the talent pool of potential successors stands in direct proportion to the organization's commitment to people and the investment it makes in developing leaders. Jack Welch's GE was far ahead of the general run of business, spending an enormous amount of time, energy, and resources nurturing the talents of its employees and transforming managers into leaders. This underscores one of the most essential leadership lessons the Welch example has to offer: *A top priority for a true leader is to build other leaders.*

"My business thrives because of boards' and top management's lack of attention to developing people," Gerry Roche, head of a major executive recruitment firm, told *Newsweek.* He considers "not working as hard to develop people as they should" to be one of the biggest mistakes companies make. "A lot of these brilliant management types withdraw into statistical, financial, rational analysis, instead of the other side, which is much harder—the characteristics of leadership, sensitivity, thoughtfulness, empowerment, people-building," Roche believes. "That's hard. They don't spend a lot of time in it in business schools either."

Welch is different because he "spends most of his time reviewing people's backgrounds for promotion. He doesn't spend all of his time studying statistical numbers for reviews."[2] Indeed, General Electric is known for its deep bench of executive talent and the numerous examples of senior executives who went on to run other companies such as Conseco and Owens Corning.

Welch's enormous and successful investment in developing human talent, his understanding of the importance of the decision on his replacement, his belief in vigorous competition, and his commitment to the GE culture and values determined the parameters and outcomes of GE's search for his successor. The process was thorough, orderly, and competitive and by design took years to reach the point of decision. It focused on internal candidates. The selection came from within, with youth and perceived leadership qualities trumping age and experience. The runners-up quickly landed big jobs at other companies, likely earning more than Immelt, the chosen successor—at least at the outset. Everybody won.

"In many ways, what Welch and his board have done is probably the most complete, thorough long-term succession plan of most any company I can think of," remarked management expert Warren Bennis shortly after the new chairman and CEO was announced.[3] In fact, while Welch veered from the style and strategy of *his* predecessor, Reg Jones, in many ways, when it came to transition, Welch clearly carried some his former boss's lessons with him.

Jones made his ultimate decision after the field was narrowed to three solid candidates. So did Welch. Jones picked someone from within GE, an individual who had spent virtually his whole life at the company and had a proven business track record. So did Welch. And he picked a youthful candidate, just 45 years old, with leadership qualities that he believed would match the test of the times. So did Welch.

Jeffrey Immelt is a GE man through and through. He met his wife at GE Plastics. His father was a manager at GE Aircraft Engines. After earning a BS degree at Dartmouth (where he was a football star) and an MBA from Harvard, Immelt soon found himself in the rough-and-tumble entrepreneurial culture of GE Plastics, which Welch always called "my favorite business."

Immelt rose quickly through the ranks during his two tours at Plastics and later distinguished himself during "combat duty" at GE Appliances, where he had to handle a huge product recall. By the time he became CEO of GE Medical Systems in 1997, he was already a Welch insider. He is credited with turning that business around, which earned him a shot at the brass ring, alongside colleagues W. James McNerney, who ran GE Aircraft Engines, and Robert L. Nardelli, head of GE Power Systems.

Like Welch, Immelt is highly competitive and full of self-confidence. "I don't worry at all about my capacity to lead," he remarked at his announcement press conference. While GE-watchers are still chuckling over the fact that both men unintentionally showed up to that press conference in the same outfits—no ties, identical blue shirts, navy sports coats and tasseled loafers—spurring quips about "Jack and Jack Junior," the two are stylistically different. At 6'4", Immelt towers over the 5'8" Welch. And whereas Welch's voice cracks and the cascade of pithy words from his mouth is punctuated by a sharp New England accent and interrupted by an occasional stammer, Immelt appears polished, smooth, and calm.

Style and tone are important to leadership—just as different melodies and arrangements can make the same lyrics sound like thoroughly different songs. But beyond the "musical" differences in evidence at Immelt's inaugural press conference, it was a struggle to detect substantive ones. Did the fact that several times Immelt emphasized the need to put the customer first—a trait he has already become known for in his prior jobs—mean that he thought there was room for improvement in today's GE, where customers are important but the shareholder is king? We'll have to wait to find out.

And wait we have—for a Jack Welch succession process did not end with an announcement of the choice. A transition period (originally slated for six months but extended so that Welch could handle what he hoped would be a merger with Honeywell) followed the announcement. During that time, Immelt served as president and chairman-elect, gradually taking on more duties while being advised by Welch and two company mentors, vice chairmen Robert C. Wright and Dennis D. Dammerman. The transition period was a continuation of the careful and thorough process of change that Welch has engineered.

As for Nardelli and McNerney, the two runners-up, there never seemed to be any question that they would leave GE after being passed over. To say they landed on their feet is an understatement—they now run Home Depot and 3M, respectively, providing further testimony to Welch's abilities as a leader who fostered the creation of other leaders.

SUCCESSION IS CRITICAL TO A LEADER'S LEGACY

AS FOR WELCH, he's pledged to "get out of the way" following his September 7, 2001, retirement date. Observers as well as some friends have commented on how difficult they believe it will be for GE's current leader to let go of the reins, citing Welch's last-minute decision to stay several months longer to handle the Honeywell merger as evidence.

In interviews Welch strongly denied these views with a vehemence suggesting he was both sensitive to the need for a retiring leader to cut loose and cut loose cleanly and struggling mightily to convince himself of that fact! "Do you think it's absolutely fair to give a guy a brand new job and throw that on top of him? That'd be irresponsible," he told the *Wall Street Journal* after delaying his retirement to handle the Honeywell merger. Staying on "was not on my mind for one second," before the Honeywell deal was announced. "This is not a guy hanging on. This story's not about me and the ancient, long-in-the-tooth CEO clinging to his seat. If anybody wants to write that stuff I wanna take them on right in the chops."[4]

For years to come, Welch and Immelt will find themselves compared and contrasted, at various times linked and separated, with each man used as a touchstone to define the other. Subsequent, possibly revisionist, assessments of Welch's performance will be influenced by how Immelt performs. For Immelt, employees, investors, partners, and media will be struggling to read the tea leaves in his every decision, action, and pronouncement.

Which decisions constitute endorsement of Welch's approach? Do any amount to repudiation? How's Jeff different? How's he doing? And beyond the obligatory compliments we expect to hear from Welch regarding his successor's act, what does Jack really think?

The world of politics, even more a personality-driven business than commerce, shows us that both the actors and spectators in the process of transition tend to define a new chapter by comparing and contrasting it to the last—even when the authors of those chapters are presumably on the same page. In presidential transitions, when control of the White House shifts between the parties, we expect the new leader to define the world anew on January 20. Everything that happened before was terrible. Everything that happened since was great. It's one additional reason why most presidents struggle mightily to see to it that they are succeeded by a kindred spirit from their own party. Aside from being able to count on a continuation of favored policies, it helps cement your legacy to have a successor praising your record instead of trashing it. Business or organizational leaders with equal concern for their achievements, policies, and legacy should factor this in when deciding how personally involved they should be in the selection of their successors.

Yet even when intraparty presidential transitions have been achieved or attempted, we still see successors playing off their predecessors' known traits as they seek to define themselves. In this fashion, George Bush became a "kinder, gentler" version of Ronald Reagan. And Al Gore presented himself to the nation as a man who would continue Bill Clinton's popular policies, but do so with integrity.

CEOs have constituencies too—boards of directors, peers, employees, customers, and investors—and in addition to the welcome and justified input they expect to have, all of Immelt's constituencies will create a certain level of background noise as they try to make sense of and assess GE's new leader. But if Jack Welch indeed trained Jeff Immelt well, the new CEO won't let himself get distracted by the background noise and he won't lose any sleep over replacing a business icon.

Like Welch he'll listen to advice, he'll draw from the culture and values of GE and those who came before him, but ultimately chart his own course—a course that's right for the business environment of this decade, not the 1980s or the 1990s. He won't try to be Jack Junior. He'll be himself.

Of course, in many ways it is easier for the new leader to take over an organization in shambles and perform a rescue operation than it is to replace a superstar in an organization almost everyone admires. In the first instance, people expect big changes. Expectations are low and any signs of improvement will be heralded as the handiwork of a management genius. In Immelt's case, all the interested parties and constituencies are looking for reassurance that he can keep a good thing going. And a few sadistic souls are waiting to see how fast he can screw things up.

It's the toughest test one can imagine—and not all that different from the one Jack Welch faced 20 years ago. If Jeff Immelt inherited the steely New England backbone from his corporate father he'll pass the test too.

Jack Welch's careful and committed nurturing of a deep bench of leaders at General Electric and the methodical way he has handled the passing of the baton to a new CEO offer a treasure trove of lessons for leaders.

Only vain and shortsighted leaders come to believe that they are indispensable and that no one could ever fill their shoes. Only selfish and insecure leaders surround themselves with weak and inadequate subordinates to make themselves look better by contrast, secretly holding information and power close to the vest. Only uncaring and unprincipled leaders shunt leadership training and succession planning aside, thinking, "Who cares what happens after I'm gone?" These leaders can't even identify that element of self-interest that should come into play—understanding that it is better to have someone replacing you who will laud your service and seek to extend your accomplishments than someone who will condemn it and unravel them.

The lesson for leaders who have poured their hearts into an organization, a cause, or a company is clear—real leaders build other leaders. If they are truly committed to their life's work, they will courageously face their own mortality and they will take steps to ensure that the values they instilled and the achievements they created will carry on when they're gone. They will do this not by creating clones or puppets or pretenders to their thrones, but by developing other leaders with the courage, judgment, integrity, and commitment to guide the organization into the uncertain and ever-changing future.

If, as a leader, you spend all day trying to make yourself irreplaceable and all night creating a cult of personality, you fail to groom other leaders, and you hold on to secrets to hobble others who may have to guide the organization in the future, you are doing a tremendous disservice to the causes and the organization you profess to care for so deeply. Ultimately you will be judged harshly by peers, successors, and by history—and whatever accomplishments you have managed will be likely to melt away.

Will you leave footprints in concrete or in the sand? Jack Welch's big shoes have made footprints in concrete in large part because of his commitment as a leader to building other leaders. It is because of that commitment at GE that Welch is able to confidently predict that choosing Jeff Immelt as his successor, a decision he called the "toughest I've ever made in my life," will also turn out to be "the best idea I've had in the past 20 years."[5]

WELCH ON LEADERSHIP: PLANNING THE SUCCESSION

- Many leaders neglect the important process of preparing their organizations for the day they are gone. Egotism, insecurity, and a desire to deny the inevitable all help explain this neglect. Taking a page from his own successor, Jack Welch was determined to avoid this common mistake.

- In fact, equipping one or more individuals with the knowledge, skills, and stature to take over is one of a leader's most important responsibilities.

- Some leaders stay out of the selection process because they want to appear fair-minded or want to avoid picking a favorite among loyal deputies. This is a mistake—for you and your organization.

- Your successor will to a large degree determine whether what you have accomplished as a leader survives. No one can expect a successor to perform exactly as you have, but will that person build on what you have done or dismantle it? Will your years of hard work be enshrined and improved upon or disparaged and wiped away?

- The best way to ensure that your organization is well led after your departure is to establish a thorough and clear succession process and foster an environment in the workplace that invests in human talent, welcomes strong deputies, and nurtures future leaders.

CHAPTER 15

WHERE ARE YOU GOING, JACK WELCH?

History will be kind to me for I intend to write it.
—WINSTON CHURCHILL

IN 1997, JACK WELCH offered one of his more comprehensive definitions of the leadership culture he was seeking to instill at General Electric:

GE Leaders . . . Always with Unyielding Integrity:

Have a Passion for Excellence and Hate Bureaucracy

Are Open to Ideas from Anywhere . . . and Committed to Work-Out

Love Quality . . . and Drive Cost and Speed for Competitive Advantage

Have the Self-Confidence to Involve Everyone and Behave in a Boundaryless Fashion

Create a Clear, Simple, Reality-Based Vision . . . and
Communicate It to All Constituencies

Have Enormous Energy and the Ability to Energize Others

Stretch . . . Set Aggressive Goals . . . Reward Progress . . .
Yet Understand Accountability and Commitment

See Change as Opportunity . . . Not Threat

Have Global Brains . . . and Build Diverse and Global
Teams.[1]

This leadership creed neatly summarizes many of the
themes and ideas discussed in this book. But it quite naturally
refrains from encompassing the examples Jack Welch personally set for the rest of us to observe and perhaps find application in our own lives. As I have also described:

Jack Welch wouldn't allow a modest background to stand
in his way, never descending into the maelstrom of whining,
complaining, blame-throwing, and self-appointed victimhood
that afflicts so many in our society today.

Jack Welch refused to let personal shortcomings undercut
his self-confidence. He is an untelegenic but still inspirational
leader in a Media Age, a master communicator with a stutter.

Jack Welch would not do just anything to get ahead. He
walked away from GE once when he believed fundamental
principles were at stake.

Jack Welch was not afraid to make tough decisions or to
buck the conventional wisdom. He put *being right* ahead of
being liked.

Jack Welch never lost his personal energy, boldness, or
commitment to his task. Refusing to bask in past glories, he
sought new challenges and took new risks until the very end.
He never became complacent in success.

Jack Welch was straight with people. He told them what he thought they needed to hear, not what they wanted to hear—and created an atmosphere in which others could talk that way to him. At any one time he was deeply absorbed in the careers of hundreds of GE executives, while using Crotonville, Work-Outs, meetings, and other communications tools to guide and mentor tens of thousands more.

And he worked hard—damned hard. Everyone likes to say they do. Being busy is a status symbol in our society, so everyone always claims to be busy. But only a few among us can muster that all-encompassing drive and passion for our work. To have done this successfully for 20 years—especially during the 20 tumultuous years of 1981–2001 as Welch did—was in itself a remarkable feat.

THE REASSURANCE OF HONEYWELL: WELCH IS HUMAN

AS THIS BOOK was being written while the breathtaking Honeywell roller coaster was plunging from its high points to its lows, I was naturally asked by friends whether the episode would change my view of Welch. A couple even wondered whether a book called *Jack Welch and Leadership* might have lost its validity given that embarrassment. But I believe it makes such a book and the attention everyone pays to Welch more relevant, not less.

Welch made a mistake—not in the desire to acquire Honeywell, but by underestimating the forces that would align against the deal. It wasn't his first. But throughout his career he refused to allow the fear of making mistakes to paralyze him into timidity and inaction.

Honeywell will be more than just a footnote in Welch's career, but his basic reputation as a leader and record as a businessperson are intact. Making such a big move at the end of his career underscored his determination to be the change agent and a willingness to take huge risks. Walking away from the deal rather than surrendering the whole store to the Europeans is typical of a man who once put his career on the line over a $1,000 pay raise.

More important than what the abortive Honeywell merger tells us about Welch is what it tells us about the future of business and whether future Jack Welches will be dynamic, influential actors in the global economy, or will they be anachronisms.

In an era of globalization, with consolidating governments and consolidating companies, is there room for the swashbuckling man (or woman) of action like Jack Welch? The kind of business leader who barks out major decisions as he charges down the hall—or, as with Welch's bid for Honeywell, scribbles out a $45 billion purchase offer in longhand and throws it onto the fax machine?

What happens to the individual worker, customer, shareholder, or even CEO when the whole world becomes one big boundaryless organization? Where does a future Jack Welch fit in such a place? How does he maneuver, make change, communicate, and influence when a prized deal can be scuttled by a government he can't even vote for and by bureaucrats he'll never have the opportunity to annihilate?

Perhaps these issues help explain why, in the wake of the Honeywell derailment, Welch's successor Jeff Immelt showed some signs of restlessness and apprehension. The *New York Times* reported that Immelt had told a French newspaper: "The most important thing that Jack can do now so I can really take the reins is to leave. I could always call him and ask for advice. But physically the business can only have one leader."[2]

Does this portend that the new leadership at GE will, as happens at so many other institutions, define itself largely in terms of how it differs from the old leadership? If so, what is to become of the house that Jack built? Back in 1990, before the final breakup of the Soviet Union, a leading management consultant described Jack Welch as "the Gorbachev of American industry, with one fundamental difference—unlike Gorbachev who talks about change, Jack Welch does it."[3]

Will Welch's company go the way of Gorbachev's nation? Will the elephant keep on dancing? Or, just as is regrettably happening in the natural world, will the elephant go the way of the dinosaur? As GE's single largest individual shareholder, Jack Welch will likely remain in a position to influence the answers to these questions—but the decisions on how to answer them will be out of his hands.

A NEW LIFE FOR JACK WELCH

AND SO AS WELCH prepares to leave the only company he has ever worked for full time, where is he going? To date he has been clearer about what he won't do than about what he will do.

He won't serve on corporate boards. "I'd be the worst board member—trying to run it all," he told friends.[4]

He'd like to advise select companies on big picture strategy, but won't take on mundane management counseling. "I'd go nuts on a six month assignment studying the inner workings of some company's cake mix," he said.[5]

And he says he won't get in Jeff Immelt's hair—even though his exit contract reportedly makes him available to GE for 30 days per year in exchange for some logistical support in his new endeavors, including use of corporate aircraft.

One thing known is that Welch is completing a book for which he received a $7.1 million advance—more than the Pope's—a sum unheard-of for a hardcover book, much less a book by a business leader. And, as mentioned, he will do some consulting on a selective basis.

For nearly 20 years Welch has preached incessantly about the need to love change, to embrace it and see it as an opportunity, not a threat. Now he has the opportunity to put his theory to a very personal test.

Welch claims to be at peace. Compared to other chapters in his life, "this is totally the most refreshing change," Welch said. "I am financially comfortable, my personal life is in good order. . . . My only job in life is to stay healthy."[6] He'll undoubtedly spend more time with his wife, Jane, in the new home they've built in Fairfield, Connecticut, and more time on the golf course beating CEOs and presidents of the United States, as he has been known to do.

Friends have been quoted saying that whatever projects and causes Welch throws himself into, he'll do it with the same energy and passion that he brought to GE. Welch says his main prerequisite for his new career is, "I want my brain to keep working."[7]

Will Jack Welch still count? Will he be listened to? Or, once stripped of GE's trappings and resources, will he lose his megaphone and fade from the scene? Welch always said that the best position to be in was to have the soul of a small company, but the body of a big one. How will he find life as an entrepreneur of sorts?

I wish Jack Welch had chosen teaching as his next career. (In fact, he has indicated some teaching is in the offing.) We really need him there—and not just in front of MBA candidates; how about college undergrads or high school students, particularly some of those we have tagged with that defeatist label, "at risk"? What parents wouldn't give their eyeteeth to have their child challenged, motivated, and inspired by an individual with the energy, spirit, and personal history of Jack Welch?

Our youth see many celebrated examples of people like them overcoming the odds to be stars in sports and entertainment. When Tiger Woods first burst on the scene, golf links, schoolyards, and playgrounds—including those in the inner city—became clogged with young golfers, each no doubt dreaming of growing up to become the next Tiger Woods. Perhaps one in a million will make it. As much as a young man like Woods is to be admired, the world that Jack Welch comes from—the world of business and entrepreneurship—offers our young people far more achievable, duplicatable dreams. That's one more reason to stop shunning our best business leaders as acolytes of greed and instead hold them up, imperfect as they are, as role models for future generations.

Welch's story provides reassurance that you don't have to be rich, connected, or cultivated, or be a model physical specimen, to attain great heights. You can have a speech problem and still succeed. You can make mistakes, big ones, and still hold your head high—so long as your mistakes don't include sacrificing your core principles and basic integrity.

This won't happen if you're a whiner or if you're lazy or if your first reaction to any idea is to tell everyone why it won't work and can't be done.

Nor can you lead or succeed without a fundamental belief in the potential residing in every person, a basic sense of optimism and an underlying humanity. The misanthrope who retreats behind a wall of impersonal technology or personal handlers may achieve great convenience and efficiency but not great leadership.

Leadership is, more than ever, a people business. It's the impression you make and the impact you have when you stand before people—coaching and motivating, learning and listening, cooperating and competing. Those who bring an abundance of passion and self-confidence to these tasks are, like Jack Welch, the leaders worth following. Even without the title of chairman affixed to his name, Jack will still rouse great interest.

And as for the 65-year-old Welch—who refuses to retire but will instead "love change" once again by eagerly starting a new career—what does he plan to do on the first morning he wakes up and no longer leads General Electric? He says he'll go to the gym. For a work-out.

NOTES

CHAPTER 1

1. Andy Serwer, "A Rare Skeptic Takes on the Cult of GE," *Fortune*, 19 February 2001.

2. John Steele Gordon, "How Did They Do It?," *American Heritage*, October 1998.

3. Theodore Caplow, Louis Hicks, Ben J. Wattenberg, *The First Measured Century* (Washington, D.C.: AEI Books, 2000).

4. Stanley Lebergott, *Pursuing Happiness: American Consumers in the 20th Century* (Princeton, NJ: Princeton University Press, 1993), p. xiii.

5. Warren Bennis, quoted at *www.quoteland.com*, under heading of "Leadership."

CHAPTER 2

1. Pamela L. Moore, "Jack : The Welch Era at General Electric," *Business Week*, 11 December, 2000, p. 97.

2. "The Global 1000," Business Week, 9 July 2001, p.73.

3. Janet Lowe, *Welch: An American Icon* (New York: John Wiley & Sons, 2001), p. 38.

4. Jack Welch, Annual Share Owners Meeting, 25 April 2001.

5. "New GE Chairman Wants Managers to be Entrepreneurs," *Wall Street Journal*, 12 July 1982.

6. Mark Potts, "GE's Welch Powering Firm Into Global Competitor," *Washington Post*, 23 September 1984.

7. "Questions and Answers: Tough Act to Follow," *Newsweek*, 11 December 2000.

8. John A. Byrne, "Jack—A Close-up Look at How America's #1 Manager Runs GE," *Business Week*, 8 June 1998, p. 90; Roger Lowenstein, "Jumping Jack Flashback," *Asian Wall Street Journal*, 16 March 2001, p. W2; David Olive, "Appraising the House That Jack Built," *National Post*, 28 January 2000, p. C01; "General Electric: You're alright, Jack," *The Economist*, 12 December 1998, p. 8.

9. Andrew Ross Sorkin, "A Rare Miscalculation for Jack Welch," *New York Times*, 3 July 2001.

10. Olive, "Appraising the House That Jack Built."

11. Thomas F. O'Boyle, *At Any Cost: Jack Welch, General Electric and the Pursuit of Profit* (New York: Vintage Books, 1998), p. 11.

12. Olive, "Appraising the House That Jack Built."

13. Louis Lavelle, "Executive Pay," *Business Week*, 16 April 2001, p. 77.

14. "GE Chairman Defends Executive Salaries," *Dow Jones Business News*, 9 April 2001.

15. *www.ge.com*—the General Electric Web site contains a great deal of historical information about the company,

its performance, and its leaders as well as details about its current business units.

16. Both O'Boyle's *At Any Cost* and Lowe's *Welch: An American Icon* detail GE's real and reputed business errors.

17. Lowe, *Welch: An American Icon*, pp. 89, 97.

18. Ibid., p. 91.

19. Jack Welch, 1999 Letter to Share Owners, 11 February 2000.

CHAPTER 3

1. Frank Swoboda, "Up Against the Walls," *Washington Post*, 27 February 1994, p. E1.

2. Janet Lowe, *Jack Welch Speaks* (New York: Wiley, 1998), p. 12.

3. Ibid., p. 13

4. Ibid., p. 15.

5. O'Boyle, *At Any Cost*, p. 48.

6. Lowe, *Jack Welch Speaks*, p. 19.

7. O'Boyle, *At Any Cost*, p. 64.

8. Ibid. p. 47

9. Ibid. p. 57

10. Potts, "GE's Welch Powering Firm Into Global Competitor."

11. Byrne, "Jack: A Close-up Look . . .", p. 90.

12. John Huey "The Odd Couple," *Fortune,* 1 May 2000.

13. Holly Peterson, "How does he feel about letting people go?" *The London Independent*, 5 November, 2000.

14. Ibid.

15. O'Boyle, *At Any Cost,* p. 57.

CHAPTER 4

1. "New GE Chairman Wants Managers to be Entrepreneurs," *Wall Street Journal.*

2. Jack Welch, 2000 Letter to Share Owners, 9 February 2001.

3. O'Boyle, *At Any Cost,* p. 69.

4. Russell Mitchell and Judith H. Dobrzynski, "Jack Welch: How Good a Manager," *Business Week*, 14 December 1987, p. 92.

5. Potts, "GE's Welch Powering Firm Into Global Competitor."

6. "GE Boss Outlaws Tyrant Managers," *USA Today,* 4 March 1992, p. 2B.

7. Debra Whitefield, "Welch Going for the Leading Edge," *Los Angeles Times*, 23 July 1987, p. 1.

8. Ram Charan, "Managing to Be Best," *Time*, 7 December 1998, p. 145.

9. Potts, "GE's Welch Powering Firm Into Global Competitor."

10. Stratford P. Sherman, "Inside the Mind of Jack Welch," *Fortune*, 27 March 1989, p. 38.

11. Potts, "GE's Welch Powering Firm Into Global Competitor."

12. Ibid.

13. Jack Welch, 2000 Letter to Share Owners, 9 February 2001.

14. Jack Welch, 1998 Letter to Share Owners, 12 February 1999.

15. Lowe, *Jack Welch Speaks,* p. 97.

16. Ibid., p. 99.

CHAPTER 5

1. Moore, "Jack: The Welch Era at General Electric."

2. Lowe, *Jack Welch Speaks,* p. 56.

3. Ibid.

4. Ivor Ries, "Boss," Australian Financial Review, 9 October 2000, p. 10.

5. Potts, "GE's Welch Powering Firm into Global Competitor."

6. Ibid.

7. Lowe, *Jack Welch Speaks,* p. 158

8. Byrne, "Jack: A Close Up Look at How America's #1 Manager Runs GE."

9. Lowe, *Jack Welch Speaks,* p. 100.

10. Deal detailed in: Robert Slater, *Get Better or Get Beaten* (New York: McGraw-Hill, 1994), pp. 77–97.

11. O'Boyle, *At Any Cost,* p. 79.

12. Peterson, "How does he feel about letting people go?"

13. Ibid.

14. O'Boyle, *At Any Cost,* p. 101

15. Jennifer Hewett, "This Quick Jack Is Net Nimble," *Sydney Morning Herald,* 23 September 2000

16. Ibid.

17. Story detailed in: Matt Murray et al, "Extended Tour," *Wall Street Journal,* 23 October 2000, p. A1

18. Olive, "Appraising the house Jack built."

19. Murray et al, "Extended Tour."

20. Ibid.

21. Sorkin, "A Rare Miscalculation for Jack Welch."

22. Ibid.

23. Pamela L. Moore, "GE-Honeywell: How Jack Stumbled," *Business Week,* 16 April 2001, p. 122.

24. Michael Elliott, "The Prosecutor Is Also the Judge," *Time,* 17 July 2001, pp. 42–43.

25. Ibid.

26. Jack Welch, 1995 Letter to Share Owners, 9 February 1996.

27. Jack Welch, 1994 Letter to Share Owners, 10 February 1995.

28. Ibid.

CHAPTER 6

1. Jack Welch, 1996 Letter to Share Owners, 7 February 1997.

2. Jack Welch, 1995 Letter to Share Owners, 9 February 1996.

3. James Kim, "Welch Thinks Small, Acts Big," *USA Today*, 26 February 1993, p. 2B.

4. Patience Wheatcroft, "Welch's Way Keeps Elephant Dancing," *The Times of London*, 13 April 2001, p. 31.

5. Pamela L. Moore, "The Man Who Would Be Welch," *Business Week*, 11 December 2000, p. 94.

6. Ibid.

7. Jack Welch, 1995 Letter to Share Owners, 9 February 1996.

8. Lowe, *Welch: An American Icon,* pp. 87–88.

9. William M. Carley, et al., "Major Challenge: How Will Welch Deal with Kidder Scandal," *Wall Street Journal*, 3 May 1994, p. A1

10. Olive, "Appraising the House That Jack Built."

11. Jack Welch, 1994 Letter to Share Owners, 10 February 1995.

12. Lowe, *Jack Welch Speaks*, p. 176.

CHAPTER 7

1. Jack Welch, 2000 Letter to Share Owners, 9 February 2001.

2. Jack Welch, 1995 Letter to Share Owners, 9 February 1996.

3. Mitchell and Dobrzynski, "Jack Welch: How Good a Manager?"

4. Sherman, "Inside the Mind of Jack Welch."

5. Jack Welch, 1995 Letter to Share Owners, 9 February 1996.

6. Ibid.

7. Peterson, "How does he feel about letting people go?"

8. Jack Welch, 1996 Letter to Share Owners, 9 February 1996.

9. Jack Welch, Annual Share Owners Meeting, 25 April 2001.

10. Jack Welch, 2000 Letter to Share Owners, 9 February 2001.

11. Jack Welch, 1994 Letter to Share Owners, 10 February 1995.

12. Ibid.

13. Byrne, "Jack: A Close-up Look at how America's #1 Manager Runs GE."

14. Ibid.

15. Jack Welch, 2000 Letter to Share Owners, 9 February 2001.

16. Ibid.

17. Byrne, "Jack: A Close-up Look at how America's #1 Manager Runs GE."

18. Mitchell and Dobrzynski, "Jack Welch: How Good a Manager?"

19. Carley, et al., "Major Challenge: How will Welch Deal with Kidder Scandal?"

20. Jack Welch, 1997 Letter to Share Owners, 13 February 1998.

CHAPTER 8

1. Slater, *Get Better or Get Beaten*, p. 141.

2. "This Boss Doesn't Believe in Bossing Around," *Economic Times,* 18 September 2000.

3. Jack Welch, 1995 Letter to Share Owners, 9 February 1996.

4. Mark Potts, "Seeking a Better Idea," *Washington Post,* 7 October 1990, p. H1.

5. Ibid.

6. Examples cited in Ibid. and Sherman, "Inside the Mind of Jack Welch."

7. Slater, *Get Better or Get Beaten*, pp. 134–139.

8. Jack Welch, 1995 Letter to Share Owners, 9 February 1996.

9. "Jack Welch Reinvents General Electric—Again," *The Economist,* 30 March 191, p. 39.

10. Whitefield, "Welch: Going for the Leading Edge."

11. Jack Welch, 1995 Letter to Share Owners, 9 February 1996.

12. Jack Welch, 1997 Letter to Share Owners and Employees, 13 February 1998.

13. Ibid.

14. Jack Welch, 1996 Letter to Share Owners, 7 February 1997.

15. Examples from Jack Welch, 1997 Letter to Share Owners, 13 February 1998.

16. Jack Welch, Annual Share Owners Meeting, 25 April 2001.

17. Jack Welch, 1997 Letter to Share Owners, 13 February 1998.

18. Ibid.

CHAPTER 9

1. Ries, "Boss."

2. Jack Welch, 1996 Letter to Share Owners, 7 February 1997.

3. "Jack Welch Reinvents General Electric-Again."

4. Peterson, "How does he feel about letting people go?"

5. Lowe, *Jack Welch Speaks,* p. 58.

6. Ibid., p. 123.

7. Mitchell and Dobrzynski, "Jack Welch: How Good a Manager?"

8. Jack Welch, 1995 Letter to Share Owners, 9 February 1996.

9. Byrne, "Jack: A Close Up Look at How America's #1 Manager Runs GE."

10. Byrne, "Jack: A Close Up Look at How America's #1 Manager Runs GE."

11. Sherman, "Inside the Mind of Jack Welch."

12. Jack Welch, Annual Share Owners Meeting, 25 April 2001.

13. Del Jones, "Welch: Nurture Best Workers," *USA Today,* 27 February 2001, p. 2B.

14. Ibid.

15. Jack Welch, 1997 Letter to Share Owners, 13 February 1998.

16. Jack Welch, Annual Share Owners Meeting, Atlanta, 25 April 2001.

17. Jack Welch, 1995 Letter to Share Owners, 9 February 1996.

18. Ibid.

19. Hewett, "This Quick Jack Is Net Nimble."

20. Jack Welch, 2000 Letter to Share Owners, 9 February 2001.

CHAPTER 10

1. Byrne, "Jack: A Close Up Look at How America's #1 Manager Runs GE."

2. "GE Chief Welch Shares Know-How in Book," *Singapore Straits Times*, 2 December 2000.

3. Mark Potts, "Workplace: A New Vision for Leadership from GE's Visionary," *Washington Post*, 8 March 1992, p. H2.

4. Slater, *Get Better or Get Beaten*, pp. 39–43.

5. Laura M. Litvan, "Leaders & Success," *Investor's Business Daily*, 20 August 1997, p. A1.

6. Byrne, "Jack: A Close Up Look at how America's #1 Manager Runs GE."

7. Ibid.

8. Jack Welch, 1995 Letter to Share Owners, 9 February 1996.

9. Ibid.

10. Described in Byrne, "Jack: A Close Up Look at How America's #1 Manager Runs GE"

11. Ibid.

12. Litvan, "Leader & Success."

13. Slater, *Get Better or Get Beaten*, p. 54.

14. Ibid.

15. Jack Welch, 1997 Letter to Share Owners, 13 February 1998

16. Olive, "Appraising the House That Jack Built."

17. Ries, "Boss."

18. Jack Welch, 2000 Letter to Share Owners, 9 February 2001.

CHAPTER 11

1. Jack Welch, Annual Share Owners Meeting, 25 April 2001.

2. Jack Welch, 2000 Letter to Share Owners, 9 February 2001.

3. Ibid.

4. Jack Welch, 1999 Letter to Share Owners, 11 February 2000.

5. Ibid.

6. Jack Welch, 1997 Letter to Share Owners, 13 February 1998.

7. Ibid.

8. Ibid.

9. Sherman, "Inside the Mind of Jack Welch."

CHAPTER 12

1. Jack Welch, Annual Share Owners Meting, 25 April 2001.

2. "This Boss Doesn't Believe in Bossing Around."

3. Daniel McGinn, "Jack Welch Goes Surfing," *Newsweek*, 25 December 2000, p. 70.

4. "GE's Jack Welch says dot-coms not a threat," *The Globe and Mail*, 27 October 2000, p. B7; see also McGinn, "Jack Welch Goes Surfing.

5. Hewett, "This Quick Jack is Net Nimble."

6. McGinn, "Jack Welch Goes Surfing."

7. Ibid.

8. Jack Welch, Annual Share Owners Meeting, 25 April 2001.

9. Jack Welch, 1999 Letter to Share Owners, 11 February 2000.

10. "This Boss Doesn't Believe in Bossing Around."

11. Jack Welch, 1999 Letter to Share Owners, 11 February 2000.

12. Huey, "The Odd Couple."

13. Ibid.

14. Ibid.

15. Peterson, "How does he feel about letting people go?"

16. Huey, "The Odd Couple."

CHAPTER 13

1. Jack Welch, 2000 Letter to Share Owners, 9 February 2001.

2. Slater, *Get Better or Get Beaten*, p. 21.

3. Lowe, *Jack Welch Speaks*, p. 117.

4. Ibid., p. 119.

5. Ibid., p. 21.

6. Ibid.

7. Ibid., p. 17.

8. Ibid., pp. 18–19.

9. Jack Welch, 1995 Letter to Share Owners, 9 February 1996.

10. Del Jones, "Why Welch did an about-face on GE's strategy," *USA Today*, 28 March 2001, p. B1—article provides these examples and describes the process that led to Welch's shift.

11. Jack Welch, 2000 Letter to Share Owners, 9 February 2001.

12. Ibid.

13. Ibid.

CHAPTER 14

1. Selection process and announcement described in: Pamela L. Moore, "The Man Who Would be Welch," *Business Week*, 11 December 2000, p. 122.

2. "Questions and Answers: Tough Act to Follow," *Newsweek*, 11 December 2000.

3. Quoted in: Lisa Girion, "GE Succession a Leadership Lesson," *Los Angeles Times*, 3 December 2000, p, W1.

4. Matt Murray et al., "On Eve of Retirement, Jack Welch Decides to Stick Around GE a Bit," *Wall Street Journal*, 23 October 2000, p. 1.

5. Jack Welch, Annual Share Owners Meeting, 25 April 2001.

CHAPTER 15

1. Jack Welch, 1996 Letter to Share Owners, 7 February 1997.

2. Sorkin, "A Rare Miscalculation for Jack Welch."

3. Mark Potts, "Seeking a Better Idea," *Washington Post,* 7 October 1990, p. H1.

4. Matt Murray, "GE Chief's Next Act," *Wall Street Journal,* 2 April 2001.

5. Ibid.

6. Ibid.

7. Ibid.

INDEX